T0243898

LET'S DO LUNCH

Pavilion
An imprint of HarperCollinsPublishers Ltd
1 London Bridge Street
London SE1 9GF

www.harpercollins.co.uk

HarperCollinsPublishers
1st Floor, Watermarque Building
Ringsend Road Dublin 4
Ireland

10 9 8 7 6 5 4 3 2 1

First published in Great Britain by
Pavilion, an imprint of
HarperCollinsPublishers Ltd 2022

Copyright © Georgia Levy 2022

Georgia Levy asserts the moral right to
be identified as the author of this work.
A catalogue record for this book is
available from the British Library.

ISBN 978-1-911682-53-0

MIX
Paper from
responsible sources
FSC® C007454

This book is produced from independently
certified FSC™ paper to ensure responsible
forest management.

For more information visit:
www.harpercollins.co.uk/green

Reproduction by Rival Colour Ltd, UK
Printed and bound in China by
RR Donnelley APS

Commissioning Editor: Cara Armstrong
Copy Editor: Stephanie Evans
Proofreader: Anne Sheasby
Design Manager: Laura Russell
Layout Designer: James Boast
Illustrator: Molly Bland
Photographer: Sam A Harris
Photography Assistants: India Whiley-Morton
and Matthew Hague
Food Stylist: Eleanor Silcock, Georgia Levy
Prop Stylist: Rachel Vere

Cook's Notes:

- All eggs are UK medium (or US large) unless
  otherwise specified.
- All onions are medium brown unless otherwise
  specified.
- Some cheeses are started with animal rennet
  and as such are not suitable for vegetarians,
  please always consult individual packets.

WHEN USING KITCHEN APPLIANCES PLEASE
ALWAYS FOLLOW THE MANUFACTURER'S
INSTRUCTIONS

Recipe Key:

(V) suitable for vegetarians

(VE) suitable for vegans

LET'S DO LUNCH

Quick and easy recipes to
brighten up your week

Georgia Levy

PAVILION

CONTENTS

INTRODUCTION

'Lunch spells potential'
Fergus Henderson

It used to be that we were all too busy being at work to give any real thought to our weekday lunches. Sure, it may have our attention at the weekend or when we're on holiday, but certainly not during the week. That was the role of the little sandwich place near the office. But now with so many of us simultaneously 'at work' and 'at home', we can no longer avoid it. Lunch is back and it's here to stay.

But I'm guessing that by now since you're reading this, you're here, you've realised this and you're reading this ready to embrace what it means to be a person who lunches during the week. It's a choice. Like meditation or exercise, you have to choose to find the time for it. But consider this: not only are you feeding yourself, but you're injecting your day with excitement, and you're taking a break by doing something that isn't typing emails or staring at your own face on Zoom meetings.

But the next challenge is what and how. Lunch is one of the best ways to brighten your day, but it involves a level of imagination. Coming up with enough dinners to keep everyone happy is a challenge enough but now lunch too? You're going to need some inspiration.

This is where this book comes in.

Decide how much time you want to dedicate to your lunch, review what you have in your fridge and cupboard, then choose a dish that appeals to you and let's go!

At the heart of this book is this lack of fuss. I'm an impatient cook and always want to eat RIGHT NOW, so if a corner can be cut, it's being cut. This means the following: no ovens are being turned on when they don't have to be, no pans will be stood over and stirred, there's no way we're waiting for anything to rise, absolutely no excessive peeling and chopping, no challenging techniques that can sabotage an entire meal and no hard-to-find ingredients you'll only use once. These recipes are all unfuckupable. But don't worry, absolutely no deliciousness will be sacrificed in the name of speed and ease. And you'll find plenty of tips and tricks to help you along the way – cooking should be fun and the journey as enjoyable as the destination.

Let's do lunch, people!

LET'S MAKE
IT QUICK

HOT SAUCE BAKED BEANS ON TOAST

This is a nifty recipe that involves only a few store-cupboard ingredients and is a world away from the canned version (but they have their place too!). Make it as spicy or as mild as you like by adjusting the hot sauce or forgoing it entirely.

Serves 4

1 tbsp olive oil

100 g/3½ oz cubed pancetta, smoked lardons or bacon

1 onion, finely chopped

2 garlic cloves, chopped

400 g/14 oz/2 cups passata

2 x 400 g/14 oz cans cannellini or borlotti beans, drained and rinsed

1–2 tbsp red wine vinegar

1 tbsp soft light brown sugar or maple syrup

A few dashes of Worcestershire sauce

1½ tsp sweet paprika

1–2 tbsp hot sauce (depending on how hot it is; just use your favourite), plus extra, to serve

4 slices of nice bread

Butter, for spreading, optional

Salt and pepper

4 fried eggs, optional

Warm the oil in a large frying pan over a medium heat. Add the pancetta and cook for a few minutes until golden and some of its fat has been released.

Add the onion, garlic and a big pinch of salt and cook for another 5 minutes, stirring often, until everything is soft.

Add the rest of the sauce ingredients, half a can of water and some seasoning. Simmer vigorously for 5 minutes to allow the sauce to thicken. Have a taste and add more sugar, Worcestershire or hot sauce as needed. Toast the bread, butter it, if you like, then spoon over the beans. Pop a fried egg on top if you're feeling decadent.

SABICH

These guys are BIG on the Tel Aviv snack scene, and you'll soon see why. The first time I ate sabich was an absolute revelation. The idea of egg and aubergine really scrambled my head, but the crunchy salad! Creamy hummus! Zingy mango! It's got it all. Sabich is traditionally eaten with Amba, a sour mango sauce, but mango chutney with a big squeeze of lemon is a very worthy stand-in.

Tip: To avoid soggy bread, slice 4–5 cm/1½–2in off the top of your pitta, then tuck that bit (cut-side up) into the bottom of the pocket to soak up the juices.

Makes 4

2 eggs

3 tbsp olive oil

1 medium aubergine, sliced into 4–5-mm/¼in rounds

½ cucumber, deseeded and diced

2 handfuls of cherry tomatoes, quartered

A big squeeze of lemon juice

4 pitta breads or other flatbreads

4 tbsp hummus, shop-bought or **homemade (p.140-141)**

Salt and pepper

MANGO SAUCE

3 tbsp mango chutney

2 tbsp lemon juice

TO SERVE

½ batch of **tahini sauce (p.139)**

Pickled green chillies, optional

Sumac, optional

Bring a small pan of water to the boil and simmer the eggs for 8 minutes for soft boiled (longer for larger eggs), then cool under cold running water.

Meanwhile, heat a griddle or large frying pan over a medium-high heat. Pour the oil into a shallow dish or bowl and toss in the aubergine so it's nicely coated. Once the pan is super-hot, add the aubergine pieces, seasoning with a little salt. You may need to do a few batches. Grill or fry for about 3–4 minutes on each side until char marks appear and the pieces are tender in the middle. Stack them up as they come out of the pan so they continue cooking a bit.

Meanwhile, make the mango sauce and put to one side.

Put the cucumber and tomatoes in a bowl. Squeeze over some lemon juice, season with a little salt and pepper before tossing together.

Peel the eggs and slice so you have everything is ready to assemble the sandwiches.

Add the pittas to the hot (aubergine) pan, grilling/frying each side until they're warmed up (you can also do this in the oven or toaster).

Stuff in the hummus, then cucumber, tomatoes, egg slices and aubergines. Drizzle over lots of the tahini sauce and the mango sauce, then top with the pickled chillies and add a sprinkling of sumac, if you wish. Very happy to be wrapped up and eaten later.

SPICY SCRAMBLED TOFU & KIMCHI ON TOAST

This is very much for tofu and/or kimchi fiends as it's all about the glorious, pillowy, bouncy texture of tofu with the spicy, sour flavour of kimchi. It takes less time than making scrambled egg and arguably is easier to make. Don't stint on the sriracha as the dish needs a good sweet kick to balance the sour kimchi.

Serves 2

2 slices of nice bread

2 tbsp rapeseed or olive oil

2 garlic cloves, 1½ sliced, other ½ left whole

350 g/12 oz silken tofu, drained

100 g/3½ oz/1 cup vegan kimchi, roughly chopped

1½ tsp soft light brown sugar

2 tsp light soy sauce

TO SERVE

1 tsp sesame seeds

Sriracha

First get your bread toasting as this scramble doesn't take long. Keep warm.

Warm the oil in a medium frying pan over a medium heat and fry the sliced garlic until soft, about 2 minutes. Add the tofu, and roughly break it up with a wooden spoon, tossing it in the garlicky oil, then add the kimchi, sugar and soy. Keep frying until they're nicely mixed in, but try not to break up the tofu too much. Have a taste and add some more soy, if needed.

Rub the remaining garlic clove half gently over one side of the warm toast, then pile over the scrambled tofu. Finish with the sesame seeds and a good drizzle of sriracha.

CREAMY DEVILLED MUSHROOMS ON TOAST WITH A FRIED EGG

Urghhh, I absolutely loathe kidneys but eating them devilled almost convinced me, though I realised it was the spicy, creamy sauce that was covering them that I liked. So here is the sauce covering mushrooms instead.

Tip: You may want to fry the mushrooms in two batches as they don't like being crowded. Make sure you've got all your ingredients ready as this cooks very quickly…

Serves 2

2 slices of sourdough bread

3 tbsp olive oil

450 g/1 lb mix of chestnut and button mushrooms, quartered

20 g/¾ oz/1½ tbsp butter

2 garlic cloves, 2 finely sliced, 1 whole

1 tsp hot paprika

1 tsp English or Dijon mustard

4 tsp Worcestershire sauce (vegetarians can leave this out)

150 g/5½ oz/¾ cup crème fraîche

A large handful of parsley leaves, chopped

2 eggs

Salt and pepper

Toast your bread and keep warm.

Place your largest frying pan over a high heat and when hot, add 2 tablespoons of oil. Add the mushrooms, in batches if necessary, and cook without stirring for 2–3 minutes until well coloured. Stir and cook briefly until all sides are coloured.

Turn the heat down slightly and add the butter, sliced garlic, paprika and some seasoning. Cook for a few moments until the garlic just begins to smell fragrant, then add the mustard, Worcestershire sauce and crème fraîche. Cook for 1 minute or so to allow the crème fraîche to thicken slightly, then stir in the parsley. Keep warm while you briefly fry the eggs (in a separate frying pan) in the remaining tablespoon of oil.

Rub the warm toast lightly with the remaining whole garlic clove, then spoon over the mushrooms and sauce. Top with the fried eggs and eat.

BACON & SWIRLY EGG SANDWICH WITH MIKE'S SAUCE

This half fried/half scrambled egg technique is perfect for those on the lazy side and actually creates an egg perfect for sandwiches (i.e. no yolk splattering, though I can't protect you from the sauce, sorry).

The sauce is brilliant in all sandwiches – it's basically ketchup's sexy, older brother. It was introduced to me by my friend Kate, whose condiment-obsessed dad, Mike, took it upon himself to create his own perfect sauce.

Makes 2

4–6 rashers of streaky bacon
20 g/1½ oz/3 tbsp butter
4 large eggs
1 tsp chopped chives or spring
  onion greens
2 large brioche buns or bagels,
  cut in half
Salt and pepper

MIKE'S SAUCE
8 tbsp ketchup
4 tsp Worcestershire sauce
2 tsp Dijon mustard
8 shakes of Tabasco sauce

Lay out the bacon rashers in a large, cold frying pan and set over a medium heat. Fry gently for 8–10 minutes, turning once, until golden and crisp. Drain on kitchen paper. Alternatively, place under your hot grill for 2–3 minutes each side.

Mix the ingredients for Mike's sauce so that it's ready to go.

For the swirly eggs, melt half of the butter in a small pan over a medium heat, crack 2 eggs directly into the pan and, with a rubber spatula, break the yolks. Swirl the yolks around to give the eggs a marbled effect, season with salt and pepper and some chives but don't stir too much as this will scramble them. Cook until the eggs are set on the bottom, about 2–3 minutes. Do not flip, instead fold them over twice, omelette-style – so they fit in your bun. Repeat with the remaining butter and eggs.

Smear some of Mike's sauce on both sides of the buns. Top with the 2–3 bacon rashers and slide your eggs on top. Eat immediately.

HOMEMADE FISH FINGER SANDWICH WITH TA DA! SAUCE

Makes 4

600 g/1 lb 5 oz skinless thick white fish fillets – cod, pollack or monkfish

75 g/2¾ oz/½ cup plain flour

1 large egg, beaten with 1 tbsp milk

150 g/5½ oz/3 cups fresh white breadcrumbs

Sunflower oil, for frying

Salt and pepper

TA DA! SAUCE

1 shallot, roughly chopped

1½ tbsp capers, soaked if salted

2 tbsp cornichons or pickled cucumbers, chopped

A handful of parsley/or tarragon leaves (or a mix), roughly chopped

100 g/3½ oz/⅓ cup mayonnaise, shop-bought or **homemade (p.142)**

100 g/3½ oz/⅓ cup Greek yogurt

Juice of ½ lemon, the other ½ reserved as wedges, to serve

TO SERVE

Ketchup

8 slices of nice bread

A couple of handfuls of shredded lettuce and/or lettuce leaves

The sauce is so-named because it takes just a few ingredients and seconds to make an absolutely magical sauce. This sandwich would be nothing without it. Feel free to buy your fish fingers but making your own is dead easy and you get the opportunity to use responsibly sourced fish. If you've got the time, use **homemade mayonnaise (p.142)**.

Tip: If you can flour, egg and breadcrumb with one hand, you might find it gets a little less messy.

Make the sauce first. Stir the ingredients together, adjusting the acid balance with a little more lemon juice if you feel you need it and add a little seasoning. It should be very, very perky.

Cut the fish into fish finger-sized pieces (or whatever size you wish; just try and make them even). Grab yourself three large plates. Put the flour on one and season very generously, pour the beaten egg and milk mix onto another, and tip the breadcrumbs onto the third. Cover the fish pieces in flour, shake to discard the excess, then coat in egg and finally in breadcrumbs.

Turn on your oven to low to keep the fish warm. Set a large, heavy-based frying pan over a medium heat and pour in enough oil to come 1 cm/½in up the sides. Get the oil hot enough to brown a few breadcrumbs in 10 seconds, and then lower in the fish fingers, in batches, and fry until golden, about 2–3 minutes on each side. Keep each batch warm in the oven while you cook the rest. Once all are cooked, season with salt and sit on top of 4 slices of ketchup-smeared bread. Spoon over the sauce, scatter over some lettuce, top each with another slice of bread and eat immediately with lemon wedges.

CHEESY EGG & SAUSAGE BURRITOS

Believe it or not, these are a little lighter than your average burrito as they don't include rice or beans. They may seem like a little effort but once you've got that salsa made, it's plain sailing. If you've got a batch of **quick pickled onions (p.146)** around, get those in too. Eat with extra hot sauce if you're anything like me.

Makes 4

4 good-quality sausages

1 tsp sweet paprika

½ tbsp butter

4 eggs, beaten

50 g/1¾ oz/½ cup Cheddar or Lancashire cheese, grated

4 large flour tortillas, ideally 25 cm/10in in diameter

SALSA

4 spring onions, finely chopped

1 ripe avocado, stoned, peeled and chopped

1 ripe tomato, deseeded and chopped

½ green or red chilli, finely chopped

2 handfuls of coriander, roughly chopped

Juice of 1 lime

Salt and pepper

Start with the salsa. Put the spring onions, avocado, tomato, chilli, coriander and lime juice in a bowl, season generously and mix well. Put to one side.

Squeeze the sausages out of their skins into a bowl and mash in the paprika. Melt the butter in a frying pan over a medium-high heat and add the sausage meat, in coin-sized bits. Fry for 2–3 minutes, until golden and just cooked through. Spoon into a bowl, leaving behind any fat.

Turn the heat down a little, whisk the eggs with a little seasoning and add to the pan. Cook, stirring, until scrambled to your liking, stirring in the cheese just before you take it off the heat. Transfer to a bowl to stop it cooking.

Wipe the pan clean and turn the heat up a little again.

To assemble the burritos, briefly warm the tortillas, one at a time, in the hot pan until pliable. Spoon a quarter of the eggs in the middle of each warm tortilla, spreading them out a little, then a quarter of the sausage and a quarter of the salsa. Fold one side of each over, followed by the top and bottom and then wet the final side with a little water and roll towards it, making sure it's nice and tight.

Return the burritos, seam-side down, to the hot pan and dry-fry for a couple of seconds to seal them, then turn over and fry the other side until slightly coloured. Halve and eat immediately.

TLAYUDA WITH GRILLED SPRING ONIONS, CHORIZO & AVOCADO

These pizza-like fellas are found on the streets of Oaxaca, Mexico and consist of a crisp tortilla topped with all sorts of fun stuff. They're perfect for lunch as they're substantial without being heavy with cheese and dough. I'd recommend using the excellent **refried beans** from Gran Luchito, but if you're not in a rush, make your own – they only take 5 minutes **(p.24)**.

Tip: This is a great way to use up leftover roast meat or greens. Anything goes with these guys.

Makes 4

2 bunches of spring onions

2 tsp olive oil

4 (about 200 g/7 oz) cooking chorizo, sliced into 1 cm/½in pieces

1 x 430 g/15 oz can refried beans, shop-bought or **homemade (p.24)**

4 large flour tortillas, 25 cm/10in in diameter

200 g/7 oz/2 cups Lancashire or mild Cheddar cheese, at room temperature and grated

1 ripe avocado, stoned, peeled and sliced

4 handfuls of rocket

TO SERVE

Lime wedges

Hot sauce

Preheat the grill to high. If making your own **refried beans (p.24)**, do them first. If using bought, follow the order of steps here.

Spread out the spring onions on a large, foiled-lined baking tray and rub each with a little oil. Dot the chorizo pieces around and put under the grill for 2–3 minutes, turning everything once, until the onions are charred and the chorizo tender and coloured. Put to one side for a moment, keeping the tray as you'll use it again.

Transfer the beans to a small pan and warm up, adding a dash of water if very dry. Next, warm up a big, dry frying pan over a medium heat and add your first tortilla. Heat until it's warmed through, then spread with a quarter of the beans and a quarter of the cheese. Keep warming just to get the cheese going, then repeat with the remaining tortillas, beans and cheese.

Divide the spring onions and chorizo between them, then put the pan under the hot grill for a couple of minutes until the cheese has just melted. If your frying pan isn't oven-proof, transfer to a baking tray. Keep an eye on the tortillas as the edges will catch quickly.

Remove, scatter over the avocado and rocket and serve immediately with a lime wedge to squeeze over each one.

REFRIED BEANS

These beans are the principle dancer in the **Tlayuda (p.22)** but as all Mexican food lovers know, they're the most versatile of dishes. And they're dead easy to make yourself, all you need is a can of black beans and a few minutes. I like to soak saturate mine in whatever hot sauce I'm currently ploughing through that week.

2 tbsp olive oil or 30 g/1 oz/
   2 tbsp butter

1 garlic clove, sliced

1 bay leaf

1 x 400 g/14 oz can black beans,
   drained and rinsed

100 ml/3½ fl oz/½ cup water

1 tsp chipotles in adobo paste or
   1 tsp hot sauce (any)

Salt

Warm the oil or butter in a small pan over a medium heat and fry the garlic, bay leaf and a pinch of salt for 2–3 minutes until the garlic is beginning to colour. Meanwhile, return the beans to the can, add some of the water to loosen and use a hand blender (or transfer to a blender) and whizz until smooth.

Add the bean purée, ¼ teaspoon of salt and the chipotles or hot sauce to the pan and simmer for 5 minutes, adding a little extra water from time to time if the mixture looks dry. The end result should be a smooth purée that falls easily from your spoon. Taste and adjust the seasoning. Remove and discard the bay leaf before serving.

HARRY'S BAR FRIED CHEESE SANDWICH

It is said these sandwiches were created at Harry's Bar in Venice. The legendary bar, established in the 1930s, is also credited with the Peach Bellini and Beef Carpaccio, so who are we to argue? These sandwiches are just the most incredibly exciting mouthful of food: crunchy, cheesy and totally taste-bud punching. As well as being a delicious and speedy lunch, they make a brilliant pre-dinner party snack – just cut them into smaller portions – and they're exceptional with a martini (what a lunch that would be!).

Makes 4

200 g/7 oz/1¾ cups Gruyère, Fontina/or mature Cheddar (or a mix), at room temperature and roughly grated

2 heaped tsp Dijon mustard

1½ tbsp Worcestershire sauce

1 tsp Tabasco sauce or ¼ tsp cayenne pepper

1 large egg yolk

2 tbsp double cream or crème fraîche

8 slices of nice white bread

4 slices of prosciutto or other ham

Sunflower oil, for frying

Put everything except the bread, prosciutto and oil in a food processor or blender (or use a hand blender) and blitz to a thick sauce.

Divide and spread the cheese mixture over one side of each slice of bread. Lay the prosciutto over 4 slices and cover with the remaining slices. Press them together firmly.

Heat a large frying pan over a medium heat. Pour in enough oil to cover the bottom of the pan generously. When the oil is hot, add as many sandwiches as will fit (you may want to cut some in half). Fry for about 2–4 minutes, until light brown and crisp (you may have to adjust the heat), then turn over and fry the other side to crisp. Drain on kitchen paper and repeat until all the sandwiches are cooked, you may need to add more oil. Cut each one in half, allow to cool slightly, then serve on their own or with a crunchy, mustardy salad..

SMOKY MUSHROOM QUESADILLA
WITH QUICKAMOLE

For this recipe, you want cooking mozzarella – it's no place for the lovely fresh version or it will be a bit soggy.

Tip: You don't want the cheese to be straight from the fridge, otherwise it will melt too slowly.

Makes 4

2 tbsp olive or rapeseed oil, plus extra for brushing

300 g/10½ oz/5 cups portobello mushrooms, cut into 5 mm/¼in slices

4 spring onions, roughly sliced

2 garlic cloves, crushed with a little salt

1–2 tbsp chipotles in adobo paste*

A small handful of coriander leaves, chopped

125 g/4½ oz/ 1 cup cooking mozzarella, grated

75 g/2¾ oz/½ cup mature Cheddar cheese, grated

4 medium flour tortillas, 20 cm/ 8in in diameter

Salt and pepper

QUICKAMOLE

1 small garlic clove, crushed with a little salt

A small handful of coriander leaves, roughly chopped

2 small ripe avocados, stoned, peeled and roughly chopped

Juice of 1 lime

Soured cream, to serve

Make the quickamole first (for efficiency, you might want to crush all 3 garlic cloves in one go). Put everything (except the soured cream) in a blender (or a bowl and use a hand blender) and whizz until smooth, then transfer to a bowl and season to taste. Put to one side.

Set your largest frying pan over a medium-high heat and once you can see it smoking, add the oil, swiftly followed by the mushrooms – the pan might feel a bit full but they'll shrink. Leave them undisturbed for 2 minutes until slightly coloured, then give them a good stir and leave them for another 2 minutes. Stir them for a final minute until they're all nicely coloured and tender.

Add the spring onions and the 2 crushed garlic cloves and cook for a minute or so until the spring onions have softened, then stir in the chipotles in adobo paste and some seasoning. Take off the heat, stir in the coriander, then scrape onto a plate and divide into four equal piles. Combine the two cheeses in a bowl. Clean out the pan.

On a chopping board, brush one side of a tortilla with some oil, then turn it over. Pile a quarter of the mushrooms over half the tortilla and sprinkle with a quarter of the cheeses, then fold over the other half to make the quesadilla. Repeat with the other three tortillas.

Return the pan to a medium-low heat and add the quesadillas, cheese-side down, ideally two at a time. Cook for around 1–2 minutes until dark golden, then turn over and cook the other side – have a peek to check the cheese is all melted. Keep warm while you cook the rest. Serve alongside the quick guacamole. Serve with soured cream.

*Not all chipotles in adobo are created equal, so if you have a very spicy one, try starting with 1 tablespoon and add more to taste. If you don't have any chipotles in adobo paste, mix 1 ½ teaspoons of smoked paprika, ½ teaspoon of cayenne pepper, 2 tablespoons of passata and a pinch of brown sugar.

Let's Make it Quick

MELTY SPANAKOPITA PITTA POCKETS

These came about when I was trying to speed up the process of making my favourite Greek spinach pie, spanakopita. I've taken the filling and stuffed it into pittas to make a really thrilling, warm, oozy, crunchy (and messy!) sandwich. I can't recommend these more, especially if you love the taste of greens as much as I do.

Makes 4

300 g/10½ oz baby spinach

4 handfuls of rocket

3 spring onions, chopped

A large handful of mint, leaves chopped

100 g/3½ oz feta

75 g/2¾ oz/½ cup cream cheese or soft goat's cheese

1 egg yolk

4 large pitta breads

Olive oil, for brushing

Salt and pepper

Put the spinach and rocket in a colander, give them a little wash under cold water, then sprinkle over 1 teaspoon of salt. Scrunch it all up with your hands, crushing and squeezing the liquid out for a minute or so until you have a messy green pulp. Squeeze out as much water from it as you possibly can, then transfer to a bowl and add some pepper, the spring onions and mint. Very finely crumble in the feta and stir in the cream cheese and egg yolk, then mix everything with a fork.

Set a griddle pan or frying pan over a medium-high heat to warm up. Pop the pittas in the toaster for a few seconds to make them easier to slice, then use a serrated knife to open them up like a book, keeping one side attached. Do this very carefully so as not to break them; a few splits here and there are ok.

Spoon a quarter of the spinach mix into the first pitta and spread with the back of a spoon, leaving just the edges clear. Repeat with the other pitta. Brush both sides of the pittas generously with olive oil. Once the pan is nice and hot, add the pittas and grill on each side for 2–2½ minutes, turning them over carefully once crisp and char marks have appeared.

Transfer to plates and cut in half or pick up and devour whole while still nice and hot.

CORONATION CAULIFLOWER SANDWICH

Here's a classic sandwich filling that happens to taste just as good with cauliflower.

Tip: Vegans, try making this with coconut yogurt and **aquafaba mayo (p.143)**. You can also make the sauce into a salad by serving it with leaves or on top of couscous. Amazing with the **bread & butter pickles (p.144)**.

Makes 4

1 medium head of cauliflower, broken into florets, small leaves reserved

1–2 tbsp olive oil

CORONATION SAUCE

1 tbsp mild curry powder

2 tbsp olive oil

5 tbsp Greek yogurt

3 tbsp mayonnaise, shop-bought or **homemade (p.142)**

2 heaped tbsp mango chutney

A handful of mint leaves, chopped

A handful of parsley leaves, chopped

2 tbsp toasted flaked almonds

2 tbsp dried cranberries, roughly chopped

1 small garlic clove, grated

Salt and pepper

TO SERVE

8 slices of nice white bread or 4 white rolls

A few handfuls of Bombay mix

A few handfuls of watercress or Little Gem leaves

Preheat the grill to high and line a baking tray with greaseproof paper. Toss the cauliflower in 1 tablespoon of oil (2 if your cauli is big), then spread out on the tray, allowing a little space between the florets, and place under the hot grill for 5–7 minutes. Add the small leaves halfway through cooking, then remove everything when it still has a little bite. Allow to cool slightly.

Meanwhile, mix together the ingredients for the coronation sauce in a big bowl, finishing by grating in the garlic. Season to taste. Once the cauliflower has slightly cooled, toss through the sauce. Use a sharp knife to cut up any bits of cauli that are too big to get in your mouth.

Pile on half of the bread slices or halved rolls before topping with some Bombay mix and a few salad leaves for crunch. Top with the other half of the bread or rolls, cut the sandwiches in half and eat immediately.

SPICY PRAWN MAYONNAISE SANDWICH SALAD

Is it a sandwich? Is it a salad? It's BOTH, my friends. This is all about texture: you've got the delicious soft sogginess of the bread, creaminess of the mayo, crunchiness from all around. The crisps are the cherry on top here, so leave them out at your own peril...

Makes 4

6 tbsp mayonnaise, shop-bought or **homemade (p.142)**

6 tbsp soured cream

2 tbsp sriracha, or other hot sauce, plus (optional) extra to serve

1 tsp Worcestershire sauce

Juice of 1½ limes, plus ½ for squeezing

400 g/14 oz peeled cooked king or Atlantic prawns or crayfish, roughly chopped if large

50 g/1¾ oz/¼ cup Japanese pickled ginger, drained and roughly chopped

6 spring onions, chopped, white and green parts separated

1 baguette, halved lengthways, then across the middle to give 4 pieces

2–3 Little Gem lettuces, leaves shredded

100 g/3½ oz/1 cup radishes, sliced

2 ripe avocados, stoned, peeled and sliced

2 packets of sweet chilli or prawn cocktail crisps, crushed up in the bag

Salt and pepper

Whisk together the mayonnaise, soured cream, sriracha, Worcestershire sauce and juice of 1½ limes in a large mixing bowl. Loosen with 2–3 tablespoons of water to make a sauce the consistency of single cream.

Stir in the prawns, pickled ginger and spring onion whites and mix. Have a taste and adjust the seasoning if needed.

Sit the baguette quarters, cut-side up, on four plates and scatter over the lettuce and radishes. Arrange the avocado slices on top and give each portion a little squeeze of the remaining ½ lime. Spoon over the prawn mayo and scatter over the spring onion greens and crisps. Give it a final drizzle of sriracha if you want, then serve.

FOUR EGG MAYONNAISES

Here are my four bids to re-invigorate this lunchbox underdog. Cook your eggs however you like them, I prefer mine soft-boiled but only just so. The timings here are for medium eggs at room temperature.

Serves 4

CHIPOTLE

6 eggs

2 tbsp chipotles in adobo paste

120 g/4¼ oz/½ cup mayonnaise, shop-bought or **homemade (p.142)** 2 tsp Dijon mustard

Juice of 1 lime

Eat with: sliced spring onions, pickled jalapeños, avocado slices, tortilla chips.

KIMCHI

6 eggs

4 tbsp kimchi, chopped, plus 2 tsp of its brine

120 g/4¼ oz/½ cup mayonnaise, shop-bought (especially Kewpie) or **homemade (p.142)**

2 spring onions, chopped

½ tsp Dijon mustard

1 tsp sesame seeds

Eat with: crispy shallots, sweet chilli or prawn cocktail crisps, extra sesame seeds.

'NDUJA

6 eggs

2 tbsp 'nduja

120 g/4¼ oz/½ cup mayonnaise, shop-bought or **homemade (p.142)**

Eat with: watercress, **quick pickled onions (p.146)**, pickled cucumbers.

HERBY GREEN

6 eggs

1 shallot, finely chopped

2 tbsp **bread & butter pickles (p.144)** or 6 cornichons, roughly chopped

2 tsp Dijon mustard

1 tsp white wine vinegar

1 tbsp each of finely chopped tarragon, chives and parsley – or whatever soft herbs you have

120 g/4¼ oz/½ cup mayonnaise, shop-bought or **homemade (p.142)**

Eat with: salt and vinegar crisps, crunchy green salad, raw vegetables.

For the eggs, bring a medium pan of water to the boil and simmer the eggs for 8 minutes before draining and cooling under cold running water. Gently roll each egg under your palm on a hard surface before peeling. Roughly chop by halving them, then running your knife through them. (Chop them more finely if you prefer.) Put in a bowl with a little seasoning before stirring in the rest of the ingredients for your choice of mayonnaise and then eat with the suggestions.

FOUR VEGETABLE FRITTERS

SAVOY CABBAGE OKONOMIYAKI

This is often called a Japanese pizza, but it's more of a fun savoury pancake. Much like pizza, however, it's endlessly customisable (and terrifyingly moreish). Try adding sweetcorn, kimchi or cooked peeled prawns. Feel free to use barbecue or HP sauce instead of making the okonomiyaki sauce.

Tip: It's best to cook these one at a time so they're easier to flip. For stress-free flipping, place a large plate on top of the pan, quickly and carefully invert the pan and plate, then slide the pancake back into the pan so that the cooked side faces up.

Serves 2/makes 2 large
    pancakes

400 g/14 oz Savoy or hispi
    (sweetheart) cabbage
100 g/3½ oz/¾ cup flour, plain
    white or wholemeal
2 eggs
4 spring onions, sliced, green
    tops reserved for serving
3–4 tbsp rapeseed oil
Salt

OKONOMIYAKI SAUCE
1 tbsp oyster sauce
2 tbsp ketchup
1 tsp Worcestershire sauce

TO SERVE
Mayonnaise, ideally Kewpie, or
    homemade (p.142)
Crushed crisps or crispy fried
    onions

To prepare the cabbage, strip the outer leaves off their stalks, roll into cigars and finely shred, then finely slice the stalks. Then shred the inner leaves, along with their stalks.

Whisk together the flour, 1 teaspoon of salt, the eggs and 100 ml/3½ fl oz/½ cup of cold water in a bowl. Add the cabbage and spring onions and mix. If adding any other ingredients (see intro above), now's the time.

Stir together the okonomiyaki sauce ingredients and put to one side.

Warm 1 tablespoon of oil in a medium frying pan over a medium heat and add half the fritter mix. Fry each side until dark golden, about 3–4 minutes, pushing down as it cooks. Very carefully turn it over when it's golden, adding a splash more oil as you turn it. If it breaks, just push it back together. Keep warm in a low oven while you cook the second one in the same way.

Transfer to plates and make criss-cross drizzles of the sauce and mayonnaise. Serve scattered with the reserved spring onion tops and crushed crisps or crispy fried onions.

SWEETCORN & CHILLI FRITTERS WITH PECORINO CREAM

I'm of the belief that if you've got fresh sweetcorn, then it's best eaten straight off the cob, so this recipe is designed for either canned or frozen, but of course use fresh if you're so inclined. Serve simply with this pecorino soured cream, or try with the **chimichurri (p.104)** and some tangy feta. I suggest you make small fritters, but to speed things up, you can make two large pancakes instead.

Tip: The key to success here (indeed, with frying all fritters) is making sure there's a generous amount of oil and that it's nice and hot before you add the mix. Try not to move them around too much in the pan so they get a chance to form a delicious crunchy crust.

Makes about 16, Serves 2–4

500 g/1 lb 2 oz/3 cups canned, drained sweetcorn or defrosted frozen or fresh sweetcorn

A bunch of spring onions, roughly sliced

2 green chillies, roughly chopped

A large handful of coriander, plus a few extra leaves, to serve

2 eggs, beaten

100 g/3½ oz/¾ cup self-raising flour

4–5 tbsp olive or rapeseed oil

Salt and pepper

PECORINO SOURED CREAM

150 ml/5 fl oz/⅔ cup soured cream

3 tbsp grated pecorino cheese

Juice and zest of ½ lime, the other ½ cut into wedges

Combine three-quarters of the sweetcorn with 1½ teaspoons of fine salt, the spring onions, chillies, coriander and eggs in either a food processor or blender (or in a large bowl and use a hand blender) and whizz until the mixture is pretty smooth (a few lumps are fine), then transfer to a bowl and stir in the remaining sweetcorn, the flour and plenty of pepper and mix well.

Stir together the ingredients for the pecorino soured cream and season lightly. Put to one side.

Warm a large frying pan over a medium heat. Add a tablespoon of oil and tilt the pan so that the base is nicely coated. Once the oil is hot and shimmering, add 2 tablespoonfuls of the sweetcorn mix and level with the back of a spoon. Work in batches, fitting in as many in the pan as you can. Fry for 2–3 minutes until golden and crisp, then use a spatula to carefully turn over the fritters (this isn't easy so be delicate) and cook the other side until golden. Keep each batch warm in a low oven while you cook the rest, adding more oil in between batches so the pan is always coated. Serve with the pecorino soured cream or other fun stuff.

KIMCHI FRITTERS

Serves 2–4

1 egg

1 tbsp kimchi brine from the jar

2 tbsp light soy sauce

100 g/3½ oz/¾ cup plain flour

250 g/9 oz/2½ cups kimchi,
   roughly chopped

4 spring onions, sliced, white
   and green parts separated

4–5 tbsp olive or rapeseed oil

3 tbsp rice vinegar

1 tsp toasted sesame seeds

Beat together the egg, brine, 1 tablespoon of soy and 4 tablespoons of water in a bowl. Whisk in the flour, then stir in the kimchi and spring onion whites.

Warm a tablespoon of oil in a large frying pan over a medium heat, and when it's nice and hot, add heaped tablespoons of the mix, working in batches, and flatten with the back of your spoon. Cook for 2 minutes or so until crisp and dark golden, then flip and cook the other side until dark golden. Check the middle of one if you're not sure if they're cooked through. Keep each batch warm in a low oven while you cook the rest, adding more oil between batches until all of the mixture is used.

Combine the remaining 1 tablespoon of soy with the rice vinegar, sesame seeds and spring onion greens in a bowl and serve with the fritters.

GRATED ROOT VEG FRITTERS

Use whatever root veg you have around, celeriac, beetroot, squash, would all work beautifully. Try stirring in a few herbs or play around with spices until you find your ideal combination.

Tip: To make two vegan 'eggs', soak 2 tablespoon of ground flaxseeds in 6 tablespoons of water for 3 minutes

Serves 2–4

½ red onion, finely sliced

150 g/5½ oz sweet potato,
   coarsely grated

150 g/5½ oz carrot, coarsely
   grated

150 g/5½ oz parsnip, coarsely
   grated

5–6 tbsp plain or gram flour

½ tsp baking powder

1 tsp ground cumin

2 eggs, beaten

4–6 tbsp rapeseed or olive oil

Salt and pepper

Place the onion and all the other veg in a tea towel and squeeze out as much moisture as possible.

Combine all the other ingredients (except the oil and seasoning) in a bowl, then stir in the veg. Season with a teaspoon of salt and a little pepper and add any other flavourings you fancy (see intro above). Use your hands to mix thoroughly; the mix should feel nice and sticky – add a little more flour if not.

In a large, non-stick frying pan, warm a tablespoon of oil over a medium heat and when it's super hot, add handfuls of the mix, working in batches, and flatten with the back of your spoon. Cook for 2–3 minutes until crisp and dark golden, then very carefully turn over (a spatula helps) and cook the other side until dark golden, adding more oil for each batch or if the pan looks dry. Have a check in the middle of one if you're not sure if they're cooked. Keep each batch warm in a low oven while you cook the rest.

Eat these with a fried egg or some grilled halloumi, or with a salad and some **watercress tzatziki (p.137).**

GREEK SALAD FLATBREAD

We all know how great tomato on toast tastes but how about tomato on flatbread?
This takes the classic Greek salad and has a little fun with it. The feta gets whipped
up into a tangy dip and the rest of the salad gets piled on top. All sitting on the
world's easiest, quickest flatbread, which takes mere minutes or two to make and
comes out soft and fluffy every time.

Makes 4

**Five-minute fluffy flatbreads
(p.155)**

½ **small red onion,** finely sliced

150 g/5½ oz feta

150 g/5½ oz/½ cup Greek yogurt

1 **small garlic clove,** crushed
with a little salt

5 tbsp olive oil, plus extra to for
drizzling

A handful of dill leaves, finely
chopped

A handful of mint leaves, finely
chopped

4 **large ripe tomatoes,** cut into
large chunks

½ **cucumber,** deseeded and cut
into large chunks

4 tbsp pitted black olives, ideally
Kalamata, roughly chopped

Salt and pepper

Make the flatbreads first, but don't cook them yet – stop after dividing
them into balls.

Soak the onion in a small bowl of cold water – this softens its pungency.
Put to one side while you prepare everything else.

Put the feta, Greek yogurt, garlic and 2 tablespoons of oil in a bowl and
use a hand blender to whizz them together until nice and smooth (add
splashes of water if too thick and don't worry if you can't get it super-
smooth). Season to taste and stir in the herbs, keeping a few pinches
aside for the end.

Put the tomatoes, cucumber and olives in a bowl with the remaining 3
tablespoons of oil and sprinkle over some seasoning. Toss together and
put to one side while you cook the flatbreads.

Set a griddle pan (or a frying pan with a splash of oil) over a medium-high
heat. Roll out the flatbreads on a lightly floured work surface to about
20 cm/8in diameter.

When the pan is super-hot, cook the flatbreads for about 30–40
seconds until char marks appear and they've puffed up, then turn over
and cook the other side.

Transfer to plates and spread over the whipped feta. Drain the onions,
then add the rest of the salad, and pile it on top of the feta. Sprinkle over
the reserved herbs, drizzle with a little extra oil, then eat with a knife and
fork or wrap each one up and eat with your hands.

Let's Make it Quick

SALAD
FOR
DAYS

SALADE NIÇOISE WITH TONNATO SAUCE

While this take on a niçoise retains all the simplicity of the original, it injects extra flashiness with the preposterously delicious **tonnato sauce (p.139)**. Drape some extra anchovies over this if you're one of those anchovy types.

Serves 4

4 small eggs

300 g/10½ oz small new potatoes, halved

300 g/10½ oz green beans, topped

1 x batch of **tonnato sauce (p.139)**

300 g/10½ oz cherry tomatoes, halved or 3 ripe medium tomatoes, cut into chunks

1 small cucumber, halved lengthways, deseeded and cut into chunks

60 g/2¼ oz/½ cup black olives, pitted

Extra virgin olive oil, for drizzling

Salt and pepper

Bring a deep pan of salted water to the boil and add the eggs and potatoes. Put the lid on so you get a nice rapid boil and cook for 8 minutes, adding the beans after 4 minutes. Everything should be tender by then (and the eggs cooked) – have a check. Drain into a sieve and cool under cold running water, paying extra attention to cooling the eggs, but don't leave everything too long under the water, as the potatoes can easily get soggy. Drain and set to one side.

Next, make the tonnato sauce.

Spread the sauce out on a large platter or divide between plates. Scatter over the potatoes, beans, tomatoes and cucumber. Peel the eggs, cut into halves and sit on top. Scatter over the olives, season with a little salt and pepper and drizzle with a little oil before serving with some hunks of bread.

HOT-SMOKED SALMON & NEW POTATO SALAD WITH CHOPPED EGG SAUCE

The most classic of combinations. Smoked fish LOVES potato. And egg. So I decided to take them uptown with a classy chopped egg sauce that is based on the traditional French *gribiche*. Hot smoked salmon would be ideal in this but most smoked fish would be great.

Serves 4

750 g/1 lb 10 oz baby new potatoes, or any waxy variety

2 celery sticks, sliced, plus any leafy tops

2 tbsp white wine vinegar

1 large head of chicory, sliced into rounds

2 tbsp olive oil

1 bunch of spring onions, sliced

200 g/7 oz hot smoked salmon or mackerel, skin discarded

Salt and pepper

CHOPPED EGG SAUCE

2 eggs

2 tbsp Dijon mustard

100 ml/3½ fl oz/½ cup olive oil

2 tbsp red wine vinegar

6 cornichons, finely chopped

2 tsp capers, soaked if salted

1 tbsp each finely chopped parsley and tarragon leaves

Bring a pan of salted water to the boil and add the eggs and potatoes. Cover and simmer vigorously, removing the eggs after 10 minutes and checking the potatoes. They should be done but keep going if not. Put the eggs in a sieve and cool under cold running water.

Prepare the rest of the egg sauce ingredients while the potatoes are cooking and put the celery (and any leaves) and chicory in a mixing bowl.

Drain the potatoes, then return them to their pan and immediately toss in the vinegar, olive oil and spring onions and season to taste. Spread on a plate to cool while you finish making the egg sauce.

Peel the eggs and separate the yolks from the whites. Mash the yolks in a small bowl with the mustard until smooth. Start very slowly dribbling in the olive oil, mixing fast as you go as if you're making mayonnaise, then stir in the vinegar.

Chop the egg white into small cubes, then add to the sauce, along with the cornichons, capers and herbs. Taste and adjust the seasoning, adding more vinegar if you like: you want it punchy and assertive.

Once the potatoes are cool, fold them through the chicory and flake in the salmon. Spread out on a platter or divide between plates.

Spoon over the egg sauce and serve immediately.

STICKY ROAST AUBERGINE WITH POMEGRANATE TABBOULEH

Ideally, you want nice wide aubergines for this so you get the maximum surface area for caramelisation. If you encounter those round Italian violet aubergines, grab 'em just for this. Take the tabbouleh ratios purely as guidance; there are no hard and fast rules here so just chuck in what herbs you have — it will be delicious either way.

Tip: Vegans, drop the feta and eat with my **za'atar pitta chips (p.153)** and a big spoonful of **hummus (p.140-141)** or **baba ganoush (p.136)**.

Serves 4

3 tbsp olive oil

1 tbsp pomegranate molasses

1 tbsp runny honey

2 aubergines (about 650 g/1 lb 7 oz), each cut lengthways into 8 long wedges per aubergine

Salt and pepper

POMEGRANATE TABBOULEH

75 g/2¾ oz/½ cup fine bulgur wheat, rinsed

4 spring onions, chopped

A big bunch of parsley, leaves and stalks finely chopped

2 large handfuls of mint leaves, finely chopped

1 medium tomato, deseeded and chopped

2 tbsp olive oil

Seeds from ½ pomegranate, plus extra to serve

Juice of 1 lemon

120 g/4 oz feta, crumbled, to serve

Preheat the oven to 220°C/200°C fan/425°F/gas mark 7 and line a large baking tray with greaseproof paper. Combine the olive oil, pomegranate molasses, honey and ½ a teaspoon of salt in a large mixing bowl and add the aubergine wedges. Smother them in the marinade, then sit them on the tray, skin-side down, and roast in the oven for 20 minutes until dark and caramelised on the outside and juicy and tender inside. Once cooked, set to one side.

Meanwhile, for the tabbouleh, put the bulgur in a pan, pour over 250 ml/9 fl oz/1 cup of boiling water and a pinch of salt, cover and boil for 5–8 minutes until tender. The water should be evaporated by now, so leave, covered, in the pan to steam dry and cool. Add more boiling water and keep going if it's not cooked yet.

Transfer the cooled bulgur to a salad bowl and run a fork through it to fluff it up. Stir in all the other tabbouleh ingredients (except the feta) and season to taste. Divide between plates and serve topped with the warm aubergine wedges.

Sprinkle with the feta and serve immediately.

LITTLE GEM SALAD WITH GRILLED GRAPES, BLUE CHEESE & WALNUTS

This is preposterously tasty, and perfect for colder days when you want something crunchy and fresh but comforting too. If you've never grilled grapes before, you're in for a very pleasant surprise – heat transforms them into intense little juicy orbs of joy. You may want to make extra salty-sweet walnuts; I find there are very few left by the time I actually assemble my salad...

Serves 4

250 g/9 oz/1⅔ cups black grapes

15 g/½ oz/1 tbsp butter

75 g/2¾ oz/½ cup walnuts, roughly chopped

1 tsp caster sugar

6 Little Gem lettuces, each cut into 4 wedges through the stem

1 large, not-too-ripe pear, quartered, cored and sliced

A few sprigs of tarragon or a few chives, chopped

Salt and pepper

BLUE CHEESE DRESSING

150 g/5½ oz blue cheese such as Stilton, Stichelton, Cashel Blue or Gorgonzola

3 tbsp Greek yogurt or soured cream

2½ tbsp white wine vinegar

6 tbsp olive oil

Preheat the grill to high. Line a small baking tray with greaseproof paper. Cut the grapes into small bunches of about 3–5 grapes, sit on the baking tray, and grill for 5–7 minutes until the skins start to split and the juices begin to run. Remove, sprinkle with a little salt and leave to cool.

Meanwhile, line a small plate with a piece of kitchen paper. Warm the butter in a small frying pan over a medium-low heat and add the walnuts. Fry gently for about 3 minutes, stirring, until the butter smells nutty and the walnuts begin to turn golden on the edges, then tip onto the kitchen paper and immediately sprinkle over the sugar and ½ teaspoon of salt, shaking the paper so that it all gets tossed together. Leave to cool.

Next, make the dressing. Put half the blue cheese, the yogurt and vinegar in a bowl and use a hand blender to blitz until smooth-ish, then blitz in the oil until you have a creamy dressing. Season to taste.

Arrange the lettuce wedges on four plates or a big platter. Tuck the pear slices in between the wedges and spoon over the dressing, then crumble over the remaining blue cheese in small chunks. Scatter over the walnuts and herbs, then spoon over the cooled grapes and their juices and serve.

WATERMELON, FETA & PICKLED ONION SALAD

OK OK, no one really needs a recipe for this, as it really is just an assembly of ingredients. So let's just call this a reminder to eat this.

Serves 4

1.5 kg/3 lb 5 oz watermelon

1 cucumber, halved lengthways and deseeded

200 g/7 oz feta

60 g/2¼ oz **quick pickled onions** (p.146)

A large handful of mint leaves, ripped

1 red chilli, deseeded and finely sliced

2 tbsp olive oil

I find the easiest way to attack a watermelon is to cut it in half or quarters, sit it cut-side down and then slice into 5cm/2in thick wedges. Run a small knife through each wedge to separate the red flesh from the white rind, cut the flesh into bite-sized chunks and transfer to a platter or divide between plates.

Cut the cucumber and feta into similar-sized chunks and scatter over the watermelon. Drape the pickled onions on top, spooning over a couple of tablespoons of pickling liquid as well. Sprinkle with the mint and chilli and drizzle over the oil. Serve immediately.

* Alternatively, to make an even quicker version of quick pickled onions, mix 2 tablespoons of red wine vinegar with 1 teaspoon caster sugar and a pinch of salt until the sugar dissolves, then add the finely sliced half-moons of ½ red onion and the red chilli slices. Toss for a few moments to combine, then leave to pickle while you prepare the rest.

SESAME SOBA NOODLES WITH AVOCADO & EDAMAME

This salad has it all: nuttiness from the soba, creaminess from the sesame, spiciness from the Chiu Chow and plenty of wholesome crunchiness from the vegetable back-up dancers. Every mouthful tastes different and that, for me, is the holy grail. This also works beautifully as a packed lunch or picnic salad as it only gets better as the sauce sinks in. It's also great with grilled steak, chicken, pork or fried tofu.

Serves 4

SALAD

180 g/6¼ oz dried soba or egg noodles

150 g/5½ oz/1½ cups frozen edamame, peas or broad beans

1 cucumber, deseeded and sliced into matchsticks

4 spring onions, sliced

8 radishes, sliced

1 ripe avocado, stoned, peeled and sliced

4 tbsp roasted salted peanuts, chopped

2 handfuls of coriander leaves, roughly chopped

Salt

DRESSING

4 tbsp Chinese sesame paste or tahini

1 garlic clove, peeled

1 tbsp sesame oil

3 tbsp light soy sauce

2 tbsp rice vinegar

2½ tbsp runny honey

2 tsp chilli oil, such as Chiu Chow, or 2 tsp sriracha, plus (optional) extra to serve

Bring a pan of salted water to the boil and cook the noodles according to the packet instructions until al dente, then scoop out into a colander and rinse under cold running water. Add the edamame to the boiling water for 3–4 minutes, then add to the noodles and rinse until cool.

Meanwhile, whisk together the dressing ingredients in the bottom of your salad bowl, as follows. Start with the sesame paste and grate in the garlic. Slowly whisk in the other ingredients, finishing with 2–3 tablespoons of water, and keep whisking until it becomes a glossy sauce the consistency of single cream. Have a taste and adjust to your liking – it should be pretty punchy: sour, sweet and spicy.

Throw the cucumber, spring onions, radishes and cold noodles and edamame into the bowl and gently mix with your hands. Scatter over the avocado, peanuts and coriander. Taste again and add another drizzle of chilli oil, if you like, before serving.

DUMPLING SALAD WITH SWEET & SPICY RAINBOW SLAW

Serves 4   (VE)

DUMPLINGS

2–4 tbsp sunflower oil

28 (or more!) of your favourite frozen vegetable gyoza

Hoisin, sriracha and/or chilli oil, to serve

SALAD

¼ red cabbage

¼ white cabbage

2 carrots, peeled and julienned

½ yellow or orange pepper, deseeded and sliced

A handful of coriander leaves, roughly chopped

A handful of mint leaves, roughly chopped

3 spring onions, sliced

4 tbsp crispy fried onions to serve, optional

DRESSING

1 garlic clove, peeled

A small thumb of ginger, peeled

4 tsp soft light brown sugar

1 red chilli, deseeded and chopped

5 tbsp light soy sauce

5 tbsp rice vinegar

2½ tbsp sesame oil

God, I love dumplings (who doesn't?) and am always looking for excuses to get them on my plate. This is one of those recipes. You can use any frozen dumpling you wish, just follow the packet instructions for cooking them. This makes quite a lot of dressing so you can have extra to dip the dumplings in. Please forgive me for asking you to use only a quarter of these cabbages, but there's a perfect recipe to use the rest of them: **red cabbage & carrot kraut (p.147)**.

Get the dumplings going first. You may need to cook them in batches or use two pans. Heat enough vegetable oil to generously cover the bottom of a large frying pan (with a lid) over a medium-high heat. Add the dumplings on their flat side and fry for 2–3 minutes until dark golden.

Carefully add enough water to come halfway up the sides of the dumplings, cover with the lid and steam for about 8–10 minutes (check the packet for exact timings) before removing the lid and cooking until all the water has evaporated.

Meanwhile, make the dressing. Finely grate the garlic and ginger into a mixing bowl, then add all the other ingredients, stirring until the sugar dissolves. Spoon 4 tablespoons into a small dipping bowl and put to one side.

Make the salad. Using your sharpest knife or a mandolin, or the slicing attachment of a food processor, shred the cabbages as finely as you can (the finer you can get, the less chewing you need to do) and transfer to a bowl. Add all the other ingredients except the crispy onions, pour in the remaining dressing and toss with your hands. Have a taste to check you're happy with the flavours: it should be sweet, salty and a little acidic. Divide between plates or bowls and sprinkle over a layer of crispy fried onions, if you like.

Once the dumplings are cooked, sit some on top of each portion. Serve with the extra dressing for dipping and drizzle over some hoisin, sriracha or chilli oil (or all three!).

SWEET & SOUR BUTTER BEAN, RADISH & GRILLED SPRING ONION SALAD

This recipe celebrates the humble butter bean. But often, living up to its name, the bean can sometimes be a bit dry. Giving it a quick warm up in salty water and coating it in a really assertive dressing brings out its best qualities. In the summer months, I would definitely chuck some asparagus under the grill with the spring onions. This would also be amazing with feta (but then what wouldn't?) or with some anchovies on top.

Serves 4

First make the dressing. Set to one side.

1 x batch of **caper & raisin dressing (p.149)**

2 x 400 g/14 oz cans butter beans, drained and rinsed

2 tbsp olive oil

1 tbsp red wine vinegar

2 bunches of spring onions

1 cucumber, deseeded and cut into chunks

200 g/7 oz/2 cups radishes, quartered

160 g/5¾ oz/10 cups rocket

A large handful of mint leaves, roughly chopped

Salt and pepper

Preheat the grill to high. Bring a pan of water to the boil and when boiling, season generously with salt and add the butter beans. As soon as it returns to the boil, take off the heat. Drain the beans and, while still warm, transfer to your salad bowl, and drizzle with a tablespoon of oil and the vinegar. Leave to cool. Spread the spring onions out on a baking tray and rub them with the remaining 1 tablespoon of oil and some seasoning. Put under the grill for 3–4 minutes, turning once until they have dark spots and are cooked through.

Add the rest of the salad ingredients to the cooled beans, except the grilled spring onions. Toss with 3–4 tablespoons of the dressing, leaving a few spoonfuls to drizzle over at the end. Transfer to a large platter or plates, sit the grilled spring onions on top and drizzle with a little more dressing before serving.

ICED SALAD WITH ANCHOVY, MOZZARELLA & PANGRATTATO

The inspiration here is the Roman classic, *puntarelle alla Romana*, a magical crunchy, punchy salad made with a slightly bitter, dramatic-looking member of the chicory family. It's soaked in iced water until it becomes super-crispy and then doused in a chilli-spiked anchovy dressing. Puntarelle is only available from specialist Italian greengrocers during the autumn, so I like making this version using the more common variety of chicory (also known as endive) so I can enjoy its pleasures year-round. I've also given it a bit more substance with some fried breadcrumbs and creamy mozzarella.

Tip: Try to use the best anchovies you can find as they are the star of the show here.

Serves 4

1 celery heart

1 large chicory or radicchio

1 head of fennel, tough outer layer discarded, any fronds reserved

DRESSING

½ garlic clove

8 anchovy fillets

A pinch of chilli flakes

2 tbsp red wine vinegar

6 tbsp extra virgin olive oil, plus extra to serve

4 tbsp **pangrattato** (p.152)

2 x 125 g/4½ oz fresh mozzarella balls, drained

Salt and pepper

Prepare a large mixing bowl with a couple of handfuls of ice cubes and fill it with cold water. Using your sharpest knife, finely slice the veg, throwing them into the iced water as you chop them, then place the bowl in the fridge. Allow to soak for at least 15 minutes.

Next, make the dressing. Finely chop the garlic, then sprinkle over a little salt and use the edge of your knife to grind it into a paste. Finely chop the anchovies into the garlic paste, then scrape everything into a small bowl. Sprinkle in the chilli, stir in the vinegar and oil and put to one side.

Make the pangrattato. Set to one side.

When the veg is nice and crunchy, spin dry in a salad spinner or gently rub dry with a clean tea towel. Transfer to a salad bowl and pour over the dressing. Toss well and have a taste – it should be perky and vibrant so adjust the seasoning and vinegar until it is.

Divide between plates. Rip each mozzarella ball in half and place on top of the salad. Scatter generously with the pangrattato and drizzle over a little extra oil to serve.

TOMATO & BASIL TRAPANESE PASTA SALAD

Pesto alla trapanese is a Sicilian sauce that combines almonds, basil and fresh tomatoes to create a wonderfully juicy, sunshiny pesto bursting with summer flavours. Here I've combined it with green beans which are great friends with both tomatoes and basil. Try to get your hands on the ripest, fanciest tomatoes you can and try to avoid the flavourless supermarket basil; it will make all the difference.

Tip: Vegetarians, you can just use a veggie hard cheese for this or omit the cheese altogether.

Serves 4

225 g/8 oz dried strozzapreti or penne

300 g/10½ oz mix of green and/or yellow beans topped and each cut into 3 pieces,

80 g/3 oz/½ cup blanched almonds

1 large garlic clove, peeled

3 large handfuls of basil leaves

300 g/10½ oz ripe tomatoes, finely chopped, all juices reserved

2 tbsp red wine vinegar

70 g/2½ oz/½ cup grated pecorino or Parmesan cheese

5 tbsp extra virgin olive oil

Salt and pepper

Bring a pan of salted water to the boil and cook the pasta until al dente following the packet instructions, adding the beans to the water for the final 6–7 minutes until they're just tender. Drain the pasta and beans and cool under cold running water, then leave to dry in a colander.

Meanwhile, put the almonds in a dry frying pan over a medium-low heat and toast, shaking the pan often, until they have taken on a golden colour, about 5–7 minutes. Allow to cool.

Using a large pestle and mortar (or a mini blender), bash together the garlic with 3/4 teaspoon of salt, then add half the basil and pound until you have a green paste. Add the almonds to the paste in the mortar, a handful at a time, and keep going again until you have fine breadcrumbs. Bash in the chopped tomatoes, or if your mortar isn't big enough, scrape the green almond mixture into a mixing bowl and bash the tomatoes to a rough pulp separately, then unite them.

Stir the vinegar and pecorino into the mix and then slowly add the oil, stirring as you go, so you get a nice, thick sauce. Season to taste and rip in the remaining basil.

Stir the pasta and beans into the sauce and eat there and then or take it out and about with you.

PANZANELLA

This Tuscan tomato and bread salad is a bombastic mouth explosion, so prepare yourself: other tomato salads pale in comparison. Panzanella traditionally uses stale bread, but I like to toast it for extra crunch. The quality of your tomatoes is key here, so I tend only to make this in the summery months when they're in their prime. This sits beautifully as all the tomato juices get absorbed into the bread, making this brilliant for packed lunches but also barbecues and picnics. It's also delicious with roast chicken or a ball of mozzarella if you want to make a bigger meal of it.

Tip: Vegetarians and vegans, you can easily leave out the anchovies.

Serves 4

1 batch of **garlic croûtons**
  (p.152)
1 small garlic clove, peeled
8 anchovy fillets
4 tbsp olive oil
1½ tbsp red wine vinegar
2 tbsp capers, soaked if salted
3 good-quality red peppers
  from a jar (I like Odysea or
  Navarrico), rinsed and cut
  into strips
75 g/2¾ oz/½ cup pitted green
  or black olives, quartered
750 g/1 lb 10 oz ripe tomatoes,
  mix of colours and sizes,
  chopped into large, even-sized
  chunks
A small bunch of basil, leaves
  picked
Quick pickled onions (p.146),
  optional
Salt and pepper

Make the croûtons.

While they cook, finely chop the garlic, then sprinkle over a little salt and use the edge of your knife to grind into a fine paste. Finely chop half the anchovies into the garlic paste, then scrape into your salad bowl and whisk in the olive oil and vinegar. Add the capers, peppers, olives and chopped tomatoes. Put to one side until the croûtons are cool.

Add the cooled croûtons and basil to the salad bowl and toss everything with your hands. Have a taste and season a little if needed – you want it to be punchy. Rip the remaining anchovy fillets in half and drape them over the top along with a few handfuls of pickled onions, if you like, before serving.

Any leftovers will keep for 2–3 days in an airtight container in the fridge.

PAILLARD CHICKEN WITH CAESAR SALAD

'Paillard' is a fancy way of saying flattened. It's super-easy and a brilliant way of cooking chicken quickly so that it stays nice and juicy. I tend to use thighs as I prefer the texture and you don't have to butterfly them, but breast is great too. I recommend baking a batch of the **garlic croûtons (p.152)** to make this a 100% certified caesar.

Tip: This can easily be done in a heavy-based frying pan – just add a tablespoon of oil to make sure you get a lovely golden crust – but don't heat the pan quite so hot as the oil will burn.

Serves 4

4 large skinless chicken thigh
    fillets or 4 small skinless
    breast fillet
1 tbsp olive oil
Salt and pepper

DRESSING

Juice of ½ lemon
1 small garlic clove, crushed
    with a little salt
1 egg yolk
6 anchovy fillets, chopped
2 tsp Dijon mustard
1 tbsp red wine vinegar
125 ml/4 fl oz/½ cup olive oil

TO SERVE

2 Romaine or 4 Little Gem
    lettuces, separated into
    leaves
50 g/2 oz/½ cup Parmesan
    cheese
Garlic croûtons (p.152)
Lemon wedges, to serve

If using chicken breasts, sit them cut-side up on a chopping board, and slice into them horizontally, about three-quarters of the way through to open them up like a book (skip this step if using thighs).

One at a time, place the chicken thighs or breasts inside a folded sheet of greaseproof paper. Use a heavy object like a frying pan or rolling pin to bash and evenly flatten the meat to about 5 mm/¼in thick. Try to avoid breaking them but it's not a disaster if you do. Rub both sides in the tablespoon of oil and season lightly.

To make the dressing, put all the dressing ingredients except the olive oil in a food processor (or into a bowl and use a hand blender) and blitz until finely chopped. Add the oil in a slow steady stream until you have a thick sauce. Put to one side while you cook the chicken.

Set a griddle pan over a high heat or heat the oil in a frying pan. When the griddle pan is wickedly hot and smoking (or the oil in the frying pan is hot and starting to shimmer), add the chicken pieces to the hot pan, pushing them down a little so they sit flat in the pan. Cook for 1–2 minutes until char marks appear (if using a griddle pan), then turn over and immediately cook the other side for the same length of time.

Once the chicken is cooked through (slice into a piece to test if unsure), transfer to warm plates to rest.

Sit the leaves on top of the grilled chicken and generously drizzle over the dressing. Grate or shave the Parmesan over each pile of salad and scatter with garlic croûtons.

NECTARINE, GRILLED BEANS & HALLOUMI SALAD WITH CHILLI & MINT

Something extraordinary happens when ripe nectarines meet green beans. I don't understand it and I can't explain it, so you're just going to have to trust me. This one is made with flat beans, but don't worry if you can only find round (French) green beans, they'll just be a bit more fiddly to grill. This is a recipe best enjoyed in the summer months when all the ingredients are at their best; it would be brilliant cooked on a barbecue, in fact.

Tip: My number one rule with cooking halloumi is to have everything assembled, ready to eat as it goes from being hot and delicious to cold and miserable in just a few minutes.

Serves 4

1–2 red chillies, deseeded and finely chopped

Juice of ½ lemon

5 tbsp olive oil, plus extra for grilling

300 g/10½ oz Italian flat or Romano beans, topped

500 g/1 lb 2 oz halloumi, sliced into pieces

2 ripe nectarines or peaches, stoned and cut into wedges

2 large ripe tomatoes, cut into chunks

A large handful of mint leaves

Salt and pepper

In a large bowl, whisk together the chillies, lemon juice and olive oil and put to one side.

Set a large griddle pan or large frying pan over a medium-high heat. Halve the beans if they look too long to fit in. When the pan is smoking hot, add the beans in a single layer (you may have to cook them in batches) and grill for 3–4 minutes on each side until char marks appear and they're tender. Transfer straight from the pan to the chilli dressing bowl, season and toss well. Keep the pan on the heat.

Dab dry the halloumi pieces with kitchen paper, then rub with a little oil. When the pan is super-hot again, add the halloumi (in batches) and cook until char marks appear and they feel floppy, about 1–2 minutes, then turn over and cook for another minute. Keep going until all the pieces are done, keeping the cooked halloumi warm in a low oven.

Add the nectarines and tomatoes to the green beans, rip over the mint leaves and gently toss.

Transfer to plates, sit the halloumi on top and eat immediately.

SALAD OF ORZO, PEAS, BROAD BEANS & ASPARAGUS WITH WHIPPED RICOTTA

This is a plate of pure spring-like joy. I've thrown in almost every spring vegetable I can name here, so don't worry if you're missing something. I'd also declare it completely acceptable to make it any time of year you want. I'm a huge fan of frozen broad beans and peas and what they might lack in fresh flavour they make up for in convenience.

Tip: Vegetarians, you can just use a veggie hard cheese for this or omit the cheese altogether. Vegans, leave off the ricotta and Parmesan, it's just the icing on the cake anyway. This is the perfect salad for picnics or lunchboxes.

Serves 4

175 g/6 oz/1 cup dried orzo

4 tbsp olive oil

A bunch of spring onions, sliced, whites and greens separated

40 g/1½ oz/⅓ cup pine kernels

125 g/4½ oz/1 cup fresh or frozen broad beans (podded weight)

125 g/4½ oz/1 cup fresh or frozen peas (podded weight)

125 g/4½ oz/1 cup green beans, topped and cut into 2.5 cm/1in lengths

175 g/6 oz asparagus, tough ends discarded, cut into 2.5 cm/1in lengths

2 handfuls of mint leaves, roughly chopped

25 g/1 oz basil leaves, roughly chopped

Zest of 1 and juice of ½ lemon, plus extra zest to serve

Salt and pepper

WHIPPED RICOTTA

150 g/5½ oz/¾ cup ricotta

1 tbsp extra virgin olive oil

30 g/1 oz/⅓ cup grated Parmesan cheese

Bring a large (because you'll be cooking all the veg in it) pan of salted water to the boil and add the orzo. Cook according to the packet instructions until al dente, then scoop out into a sieve (keep the cooking water) and rinse briefly in cold water. Transfer to a large mixing bowl, stir through a tablespoon of oil to prevent it sticking and leave to cool further.

While the orzo is cooking, warm 3 tablespoons of oil in a wide frying pan and fry the spring onion whites and the pine kernels with a pinch of salt for 3–4 minutes until the onions are soft and the pine kernels are beginning to colour. Keep the heat very low while you cook the veg.

Return the orzo water to the boil (you may want to top up the pan with boiling water) and add the broad beans, peas, green beans and asparagus. Cook for 4–5 minutes (more if using frozen) until tender (best to test a green bean as they take the longest), then drain and immediately stir into the warm spring onion pan. Turn up the heat to medium and add half the herbs and the spring onion greens and keep cooking, stirring, for a minute or two to give the veg a chance to absorb the flavours.

Scrape the veg into the orzo bowl, stir in the remaining herbs, add the lemon zest and squeeze in the juice. Have a taste and adjust the seasoning. Put to one side for a moment. (You may want to add more lemon juice once it's cooled a little.)

In a separate bowl, whip the ricotta with 2 tablespoons of water and the oil and keep whipping until it's fluffy. Add the Parmesan and some seasoning and whip until combined.

Transfer the salad to plates and dollop over the whipped ricotta. Grate over some extra lemon zest just before serving.

CAULIFLOWER ALLA PUTTANESCA WITH MOZZARELLA & GARLICKY TOAST

We've all tried that ingenious empty-cupboard dish affectionately known as 'Tart's Spaghetti', but have you tried the sauce smothered on cauliflower? NO? Well, fix that. Grilling cauliflower came as quite a revelation to me: charred on the edges and a little crunch left at its heart.

Tip: Vegetarians, you can definitely drop the anchovies without losing the spirit of this dish. Check that your mozzarella/burrata is veggie-friendly.

Serves 4

1 large head of cauliflower, florets separated, the stem cut into even-sized wedges and any small leaves reserved

3–4 tbsp olive oil

2 garlic cloves, sliced

6 anchovy fillets, chopped

¼–½ tsp chilli flakes (depending on their strength and your enjoyment)

200 g/7 oz/1 cup passata

50 g/1¾ oz/⅓ cup pitted black or green olives, chopped

2 tbsp capers, soaked if salted

½ tsp dried oregano

A large handful of parsley leaves, chopped

2 x 125 g/4½ oz fresh mozzarella or burrata balls, drained

Salt and pepper

Zest of 1 lemon, to serve

GARLICKY TOAST

4 slices of sourdough bread

1 small garlic clove, peeled

Extra virgin olive oil, for drizzling

Preheat the grill to high and line a baking tray with greaseproof paper. Toss the cauliflower pieces in 1 tablespoon of oil (2 if your cauli is big), then spread out on the tray, making sure there's a little space between the pieces, and put under the hot grill for 6–8 minutes. Add the small leaves halfway through cooking.

Meanwhile, warm the remaining 2 tablespoons of oil in a large frying pan over a medium-low heat and add the garlic, anchovies and chilli flakes. Cook for a couple of minutes to soften the garlic, then add the passata, olives, capers and oregano and simmer for 5–7 minutes to reduce the passata slightly – it may look a bit dry but that's how you know the passata is cooking.

Once the cauliflower is nicely burnt on the edges but still has a little bite in the middle, remove the tray from the grill. Taste the tomato sauce and season if needed, then turn up the heat and add the cauliflower along with the parsley. Stir through the sauce for a minute or so, enough to coat the cauli in the sauce.

Toast the sourdough and rub each slice lightly with the garlic, then drizzle over some oil and sprinkle with a tiny bit of salt. Place a slice on each plate, then spoon the cauliflower onto the plates. Rip each mozzarella in half and sit on the plates. Grate over a little lemon zest and finish with a drizzle of oil.

BIG BOWL ENERGY

SUPER GREENS PASTA WITH BURRATA

This is possibly one of the easiest, most wholesome pasta sauces in existence. I love to make it when I need a pasta hit but also crave an injection of dark, leafy greens. It is also the perfect dish for that bottle of fancy oil you might have in the back of your cupboard; nothing brings out olive oil's greatness more than a leafy veg. You can use almost any green leaf here ... cavolo nero is the classic option, but Savoy cabbage, cime di rapa (broccoli rabe) or spinach all work well – even those mixed bags of watercress, spinach and rocket sold in supermarkets.

Some creamy burrata ripped over the dish is truly a thrilling experience but not essential; a little extra Parmesan would do the job beautifully too.

Serves 4

500 g/1 lb 2 oz cavolo nero, or any brassica, stripped of stems

2 garlic cloves, peeled

350 g/12 oz dried spaghetti, farfalle or penne

40 g/1½ oz/⅓ cup pine kernels or blanched almonds

4 tbsp extra virgin olive oil, plus extra, to serve

75 g/2¾ oz/¾ cup grated Parmesan cheese

2 x 125 g/4½ fresh burrata or mozzarella balls, drained

Salt and pepper

Bring a large pan of salted water to the boil. Add the cavolo leaves and garlic and cook until tender, about 5–6 minutes. Scoop the cavolo and garlic into a colander and return the water to the boil. Add the pasta and cook until al dente according to the packet instructions.

Meanwhile, put the cavolo and garlic in a food processor or blender along with the pine kernels. Blitz until fine, then add a big splash of water from the pasta pan and with the motor running, add the oil, whizzing until you have a fine purée.

Drain the cooked pasta, reserving a cupful of the cooking water, and return the pasta to the pan along with the sauce. Put over a medium heat, then stir in the Parmesan and season to taste. Stir well, adding some of the reserved pasta water if it's looking dry – you want it very saucy. Transfer to plates, drizzle with a little extra oil and rip over burrata.

SUPER-QUICK SAUSAGE & CREAM PASTA

This has all the deliciousness of bolognese and it'll only take you 20 minutes of cooking. Plus there's the added benefit of hardly any chopping. The special trick here is frying the sausages like hamburgers, it means you get a lovely golden colour on the outside but the middle stays juicy. You then break them up into sexy little nuggets. Try and get sausages with a high meat content as anything too bready won't be happy in this context.

Serves 4

2 tbsp olive oil

400 g/14 oz Italian-style pork sausages, skins discarded

2 garlic cloves, sliced

350 g/12 oz dried rigatoni, penne or fusilli

1 heaped tsp fennel seeds

A big pinch of chilli flakes

1 x 400 g/14 oz plum tomatoes, drained and rinsed

75 ml/2½fl oz/5 tbsp double cream

Grated Parmesan cheese, to serve

Salt and pepper

Put a large pan of salted water on to boil for the pasta.

Warm a tablespoon of olive oil in a large frying pan over a medium heat. Shape the sausage meat into 4 hamburger shapes and once the oil is hot, add them to the pan. Cook for 3–4 minutes until dark and golden, then turn over to cook the other side for another 3 minutes, adding the garlic for the last couple of minutes or so, cooking until it colours.

Add the pasta to the boiling water and cook until al dente following the packet instructions.

Once both sides of the sausage 'burgers' are looking delicious and the garlic is tender, add the fennel seeds and chilli and give them a sec to warm through.

Turn the heat down a little and add the tomatoes to the pan, breaking them up with your spoon. Simmer for 5–6 minutes until the tomatoes are slightly reduced, then add 75ml/2½fl oz/5 tbsp of water and the cream to your pan and scrape up any sticky tomato bits. Keep simmering until the pasta is ready.

Once the pasta is a minute or so from being cooked, break up the sausage 'burgers' with your spoon into small nuggets. Check the seasoning and adjust to taste.

Once al dente, drain the pasta, reserving a cupful of the cooking water. Add the pasta to the pan with a good splash of the reserved pasta water, turn up the heat and cook hard and fast for a minute or so to get the sauce into the pasta.

Transfer to warm plates and cover in grated Parmesan before serving.

BROCCOLI & ANCHOVY FARFALLE

This is one of those dishes that thrills me every time. In fact, I think it's probably the nicest thing you can do to a head of broccoli. It's absolutely foolproof too, as cooking times and quantities are totally flexible. Want more garlic? DO IT. Need more chilli? DON'T LET ME STOP YOU. I like it most with super-flavoursome purple sprouting broccoli, but tenderstem or regular broccoli is fine too. As is the spectacular-looking romanesco broccoli. I'd highly recommend serving this with one of the **pangrattato recipes (p.152)**.

Serves 4

350 g/12 oz purple sprouting, tenderstem or regular broccoli, cut into small florets, and stems roughly sliced

350 g/12 oz dried farfalle, orecchiette or casarecce

4 tbsp olive oil

2 garlic cloves, finely sliced

3 tbsp pine kernels

8 anchovy fillets, chopped

A pinch of chilli flakes

1 heaped tsp fennel seeds

A good knob of butter

2 handfuls of parsley leaves, chopped

Salt and pepper

TO SERVE
1 batch of **pangrattato, optional (p.152)**

Bring a pan of salted water to the boil and briefly blanch the broccoli for 2–4 minutes until tender. Scoop into a colander to steam dry and return the pan to the boil, then cook the pasta until al dente following the packet instructions.

Warm the olive oil in a large frying pan over a medium-low heat and briefly fry the garlic and pine kernels until the garlic becomes sticky but not coloured. Add the anchovies, chilli and fennel seeds and squash the anchovies into the pan until they are absorbed into the oil. Add the broccoli to the pan and toss everything together so it's coated in the sauce. Add a big splash of water and the butter and let the sauce bubble away until the liquid has cooked off and the broccoli has absorbed all the sauce's flavours. Stir in the parsley.

Once al dente, drain the pasta, reserving a cupful of the cooking water. Add the pasta to the sauce over the heat and loosen with a little of the reserved pasta water so the sauce clings to the pasta. Taste, and adjust seasoning if necessary. Transfer to plates and serve immediately, ideally sprinkled with some pangrattato.

SPINACH & RICOTTA PASTA

You've seen this combo IN your pasta, but did you know it's just as good ON your pasta? And it's possibly the easiest and quickest sauce to grace your plates with fewer ingredients than you have fingers on your hands. Get that pasta water rolling, whip up your sauce and you're eating in under 12 minutes. Speedy or what?

Tip: This would be amazing with the **chilli & lemon pangrattato (p.153)**.

Serves 4

350 g/12 oz dried penne,
    conchiglie or casarecce
400 g/14 oz fresh spinach or
    defrosted frozen spinach
250 g/9 oz/1 cup ricotta
4 tbsp grated pecorino or
    Parmesan cheese, plus extra
    to serve
A few gratings of nutmeg
Salt and pepper

TO SERVE
Zest of 1 lemon
Olive oil

Bring a deep pan of salted water to the boil and cook the pasta until al dente following the packet instructions.

Meanwhile, cram the spinach and a pinch of salt into a separate saucepan with a lid and put over a medium heat to steam. Cook, stirring once or twice, until the spinach has just wilted, then drain and squeeze out the liquid by pushing it against the side of the sieve. Transfer to a chopping board and finely chop, then transfer to a bowl.

Stir in the ricotta, then fold in the grated cheese, a few gratings of nutmeg and a generous amount of seasoning.

Drain the cooked pasta, reserving a cupful of the cooking water. Tip the pasta into the sauce (or the other way round if easier) along with a good splash of the reserved pasta water and simmer for a couple of minutes to get everything to mingle. Serve with extra cheese, a little lemon zest and a drizzle of oil, then eat.

TOMATO, MASCARPONE & ROCKET PASTA

This is my fall-back pasta when I have no time but want a big bowl of comfort. It's got everything you want in a mouthful: tangy-sweet tomatoes, heady garlic, creamy mascarpone and peppery rocket. The sauce only takes as long as the pasta to cook, which makes for maximum efficiency. Any leftovers, I insist you use in a spaghetti frittata (see **p.127, the 'nduja, mascarpone & spaghetti frittata,** for a guide).

Tip: Rinsing your canned tomatoes means you get just the pure, juicy tomato, not the gunky, sweet sauce that surrounds them and slows down their cooking.

Serves 4

- 3 tbsp olive oil, plus extra for drizzling
- 3 garlic cloves, sliced
- 2 x 400 g/14 oz cans plum tomatoes, drained and rinsed, or 800 g/1 lb 12 oz/4 cups passata
- 350 g/12 oz dried spaghetti, tagliatelle, casarecce or penne
- 120 g/4¼ oz/½ cup mascarpone
- 120 g/4¼ oz/8 handfuls of rocket
- Grated Parmesan or pecorino cheese, to serve
- Salt and pepper

Get the tomato sauce going first. Warm the olive oil in a wide pan or frying pan over a medium heat and gently fry the garlic until it becomes sticky and is coloured on the edges. Add the tomatoes, breaking them up with your spoon. Add some seasoning and leave the tomatoes to fry in the garlicky oil for at least 10 minutes while you cook your pasta. Stir often, adding splashes of water if the tomatoes look dry.

Bring a large pan of salted water to the boil and cook the pasta until al dente following the packet instructions.

Drain the cooked pasta, reserving a cupful of the cooking water. Tip the pasta into the sauce (or the other way round if easier) along with a good splash of the reserved pasta water so the sauce comes halfway up the pasta. Simmer vigorously, stirring so the pasta absorbs the sauce, then fold in the mascarpone. After a few seconds, when nice and hot, take the pan off the heat and fold in the rocket. Transfer to plates, sprinkle with some grated Parmesan, add a drizzle of oil and serve.

TUNA PUTTANESCA

This is my favourite throw-it-all-in sauce, perfect for when you don't have much in your fridge. Also, this makes the ultimate cold pasta salad – just use a salad-friendly shape such as penne or fusilli.

Serves 4

3 tbsp olive oil, plus extra for drizzling

1 red onion, chopped

4 anchovy fillets, chopped

2 garlic cloves, chopped

350 g/12 oz dried fusilli, spaghetti or penne

½–¾ tsp chilli flakes

2 tbsp capers, soaked if salted

60 g/2¼ oz/½ cup pitted black olives, roughly chopped

400 g/14 oz/2 cups passata

2 x cans high-quality tuna, about 160 g/5¾ oz each (110 g/3¾ oz drained weight), drained

2 handfuls of parsley leaves, chopped

Salt and pepper

Bring a large pan of salted water to the boil.

Warm the olive oil in a frying pan over a medium heat and add the onion and a pinch of salt. Cook, stirring, for 8 minutes until soft, then add the anchovies and garlic and cook for another 2 minutes or so until the garlic begins to colour on the edges.

Add the pasta to the boiling water and cook until al dente following the packet instructions.

Add the chilli, capers, olives and passata to the onion and vigorously fry to reduce the sauce, stirring, while the pasta cooks. If the sauce begins to look dry, add splashes of water and keep going until the pasta is cooked. Just before you drain it, stir the tuna into the tomato sauce to warm through, trying not to break it up too much.

Drain the cooked pasta, reserving a cupful of the cooking water. While over the heat, stir the pasta and parsley into the sauce, adding splashes of the reserved pasta water to loosen it. Serve immediately with a little extra oil drizzled over.

AMATRICIANA

Salsa all'amatriciana is a classic Italian sauce and is so much more than the sum of its parts; the smoky bacon fat mixed with chilli and tomato is a killer combination.

Serves 4

3 tbsp olive oil

250 g/9 oz pancetta or guanciale, finely sliced

½–¾ tsp chilli flakes

4 garlic cloves, finely chopped

700 g/1 lb 9 oz/3½ cups passata

350 g/12 oz dried spaghetti

65 g/2¼ oz/½ cup grated pecorino or Parmesan cheese, plus extra to serve

Salt and pepper

Bring a large pan of salted water to the boil.

Warm the oil in a large frying pan over a medium heat. Add the pancetta and gently fry until it is crisp and golden and has released most of its fat, about 4 minutes. Add the chilli and garlic and cook, stirring, until the garlic begins to colour on the edges, about 2–3 minutes. Add the passata and simmer for another 10–15 minutes while you cook the pasta in the boiling water until al dente following the packet instructions.

Drain the cooked pasta, reserving a cupful of the cooking water. Still over the heat, stir the pasta and the grated pecorino into the sauce and add a few splashes of the reserved pasta water and stir until you have a lovely loose sauce. Check and adjust the seasoning.

Take off the heat, transfer to bowls and serve with a little extra pecorino grated on top.

SICILIAN STORE-CUPBOARD SARDINE PASTA

This is a great store-cupboard pasta sauce for those who love fishy fish (you know who you are!). It has substance, sweetness and saltiness all rolled into one magnificent mouthful and I highly recommend it when you're looking for an easy-breezy pasta sauce.

Serves 4

50 g/1¾ oz/½ cup sultanas or raisins

A big pinch of saffron threads

350 g/12 oz dried spaghetti or linguine

3 tbsp olive oil, plus extra for drizzling

1 onion, finely sliced

2 garlic cloves, finely chopped

1 heaped tsp fennel seeds

½ tsp chilli flakes

50 g/1¾ oz/½ cup flaked almonds or pine kernels, toasted

2 x 120 g/4¼ oz cans sardines in olive oil

2 large handfuls of parsley leaves, chopped

Salt and pepper

Cover the sultanas and saffron with 120ml/4fl oz/½ cup of boiling water and put to one side.

Warm the olive oil in a frying pan over a medium heat and fry the onion with a big pinch of salt for 10–12 minutes until soft, adding the garlic, fennel seeds, chilli and almonds for the last 2 minutes.

Add the sultanas, saffron and soaking liquid to make a nice wet sauce – add a little pasta cooking water if needed. Season to taste and bring to a simmer, then keep simmering while you wait for the pasta.

Bring a large pan of salted water to the boil and cook the pasta until al dente following the packet instructions.

Drain the cooked pasta, reserving a cupful of the cooking water. Add the drained pasta to the sauce in the frying pan, then remove the sardines from the oil, separate the flesh from the bones and flake into the pasta, along with the parsley and a few splashes of the reserved pasta water so you have a nice loose sauce.

Transfer to plates, drizzle with a little extra oil and serve.

HOT SMOKED SALMON PASTA WITH CREME FRAICHE & PEAS

This just couldn't be any quicker or easier to make. Yet the outcome is the most colourful, textured, creamy plate of wonderful satisfaction. It is also sensational as a cold pasta salad for your lunchbox, just let the pasta cool before mixing everything together.

Serves 4

350 g/12 oz dried orecchiette

3 tbsp olive oil

1 bunch of spring onions, sliced

250 g/9 oz frozen peas

200 g/7 oz full-fat crème fraîche

200 g/7 oz hot smoked salmon or smoked mackerel, skinless

Zest of 1 lemon, plus the wedges, to serve

A big handful of dill or parsley leaves, roughly chopped

Salt and pepper

Bring a large pan of salted water to the boil and start cooking your pasta.

Meanwhile, in a medium pan over a medium heat, warm the oil and fry the spring onions for a couple of minutes until soft, then add the peas and a couple of splashes of water. Simmer until the peas are tender.

Turn the heat down to low, then stir in the crème fraîche, flake in the salmon, zest in the lemon and stir through the herbs. Add a good amount of pepper here too. Take off the heat until your pasta is ready.

Once al dente, drain the pasta, reserving a cupful of the cooking water.

Return the pasta to its pan and gently stir through the sauce, adding a few splashes of the reserved pasta water until you have a lovely saucey sauce. Transfer to plates. Cut the lemon into quarters and pop one onto each plate for people to squeeze over themselves before serving.

CAVOLO NERO MINESTRONE

I'm completely passionate about this soup, I don't think there's even enough room on this page for me to describe all the reasons why. Here's what I do have room to tell you. I make my minestrone nice and thick but do add more water if you don't. And totally throw in some pasta. This gets better and better as the days pass, so make a big batch. Eat with garlicky toast or stir in stale bread to make a Tuscan *Ribollita*. It also freezes really well.

Tip: I usually make this with canned beans BUT if you are able to plan in extra time to soak and cook some dried beans, adding their cooking liquid to this soup takes it to whole new dimensions.

Serves 4

4 tbsp olive oil

1 onion, chopped

1 carrot, peeled and chopped

2 celery sticks, chopped

3 garlic cloves, chopped

300 g/10½ oz cavolo nero or Savoy cabbage (or a mix), stems removed

1 x 225 g/8 oz can plum tomatoes, drained and rinsed

2 x 400 g/14 oz cans borlotti or cannellini beans (or 1 can of each), drained and rinsed, or 700 g/1 lb 5 oz freshly cooked beans

Salt and pepper

Extra virgin olive oil, to serve

Warm the olive oil in a heavy-based pan over a medium-low heat and add the onion, carrot, celery, garlic and a big pinch of salt. Cover and cook, stirring occasionally, for 12–15 minutes until the veg is completely soft and sweet.

Meanwhile, bring a deep pan of salted water to the boil and blanch the cavolo until tender, about 5–6 minutes, then take off the heat, drain (I like to roughly chop it with scissors while in the sieve, but keep the water.

Stir the tomatoes into the veg, breaking them up with a spoon, and cook for a further 10 minutes. Add the beans (and any cooking water if cooked from fresh) and cook for a further few minutes. Using a hand blender, purée about a quarter of the mix while still in the pan to thicken it up (or remove 3 ladlefuls and blitz in a blender), then return to the pan.

Scoop in the cavolo and pour over enough of its cooking water to just cover the veg. Season, then bring to a simmer for 5-10 minutes to unite everything, then turn off the heat. Transfer to bowls and drizzle each portion with plenty of nice extra virgin olive oil. Keeps for a week in the fridge and will just get better and better.

MOROCCAN-SPICED CHICKPEA SOUP

This is the most perfect lunch for a cold grim day when you need warming from the inside. Loads of spices, wholesome chickpeas and kale, it will also fill you up for hours.

Tip: Do go ahead and make a big batch if you have the time as this freezes really well – I like to keep portions of soup in my freezer for those days when I can't stretch to cooking a lunch.

Serves 4

4 tbsp olive oil

1 onion, chopped

2 carrots, peeled and chopped

3 garlic cloves, chopped

2 tsp ground cumin

½ tsp ground cinnamon

1 tsp sweet paprika

¼ tsp chilli flakes

1 x 400 g/14 oz can plum tomatoes, drained and rinsed

2 x 400 g/14 oz cans chickpeas, drained and rinsed

300 g/10½ oz chopped kale

A small bunch of coriander, chopped

Salt and pepper

Harissa, to serve

Warm the oil in a heavy-based pan over a medium-low heat and add the onion, carrots, garlic and a big pinch of salt. Cover and cook, stirring occasionally, for 12–15 minutes until the veg is completely soft and sweet.

Add the spices and cook for another minute or so to warm them through, then stir in the tomatoes, breaking them up with a spoon, followed by the chickpeas and cook for a further 10 minutes.

Using a hand blender, purée about a quarter of the mix while still in the pan to thicken it up (or remove 3 small ladlefuls and blitz in a blender, then return to the pan).

Add the kale and pour over 1.25L boiling water to just cover the kale. Season and bring back to the boil, then simmer for 5-8 minutes or until the kale is tender. Stir through the coriander, then transfer to bowls and dollop a small spoonful of harissa into each bowl.

SUPER-QUICK MISO UDON WITH CABBAGE & SHIITAKE MUSHROOMS

I eat a version of this relentlessly during autumn and winter, sometimes changing the noodles to buckwheat or flat rice noodles, the broth to chicken and throwing in whatever greens I have in my fridge. Almost always with a spoon of magical Chiu Chow chilli oil, though. This is my ultimate no-imagination-but-always-hits-the-spot lunch.

Serves 4

1 tbsp sesame oil, plus extra to serve

1 tbsp vegetable oil

2 garlic cloves, finely chopped

A thumb of ginger, peeled and finely chopped

A bunch of spring onions, cut into 1 cm/½ in lengths

300 g/10½ oz fresh shiitake mushrooms, quartered

2 tbsp light soy sauce, plus extra to serve

4 tbsp red or white miso paste

1 hispi (sweetheart) cabbage, finely shredded, core discarded

400 g/14 oz fresh udon or other noodles

Salt

Chiu Chow chilli oil, to serve

Bring a large pan of lightly salted water to the boil.

Warm the oils in a large frying pan over a medium heat and add the garlic, ginger and spring onions. Stir-fry for a few seconds until they begin to sizzle, then scoop the garlic etc into a small bowl, leaving behind the oil, and put to one side for a moment. Add the mushrooms and stir-fry for 2–4 minutes, until they begin to colour on the edges and soften. The pan may be a bit crowded until they begin to soften.

Once the mushrooms are tender, return the garlic etc to the pan, add the soy sauce and stir-fry for a moment until it all evaporates, then stir in the miso paste. Take off the heat and put to one side.

Meanwhile, add the cabbage to the pan of boiling water and, as soon as it comes back to the boil, cook for about 1–2 minutes, then add the udon noodles and cook for a further minute or so until they're hot.

Using tongs, divide the cabbage and noodles between warm bowls, reserving the cooking water. Divide the miso mushrooms between the bowls, pour over the reserved cooking water and stir to dissolve the miso in the hot water. Give everyone extra sesame oil, soy and chilli oil to season their bowls, and serve immediately.

GAZPACHO

This is the simplest of recipes, so it really needs the best ingredients. Try to get your hands on long, pointed and thinner-skinned peppers, ideally Romano, and the juiciest tomatoes money can buy. The more powerful your blender, the smoother and creamier this will be.

Tip: For both of these **gazpacho recipes (p.92)**, roughly chop the vegetables before adding to the blender to make it more efficient. You may need to do this in batches, depending on the size of your blender.

Serves 4

600 g/2 lb super-ripe big red tomatoes, cores discarded

200 g/7 oz red peppers, deseeded

½ small red onion

1 garlic clove, finely choppped

1 large cucumber, peeled and deseeded

75 ml/2½ fl oz/ 5 tbsp extra virgin olive oil

2 tbsp white wine vinegar

175 ml/6 fl oz/¾ cup water

Salt and pepper

TO SERVE
Cucumber slices
Garlic croûtons (p.152)

Put everything in a blender or food processor with ½ teaspoon of salt and some pepper and blitz until smooth. Adjust the seasoning to taste, you may want to add more vinegar and maybe some more salt.

Chill in the fridge for at least one hour before serving in bowls topped with cucumber slices and garlic croûtons.

GREEN GAZPACHO

A green version of the red classic. If the red one is Spain in a bowl, this is Mexico. It shares all the qualities of the original – amazing mouthfeel, super-wholesome ingredients and bright flavours. The cashews add a lovely creaminess and take the edge off all the green things.

Serves 4

50 g/1¾ oz/½ cup raw cashews, soaked in 100 ml/3½fl oz/½ cup water for at least an hour

1 small garlic clove, chopped

2 large cucumbers, peeled and deseeded

A bunch of spring onions

2 green eating apples, such as Granny Smith, peeled and cored

2 green peppers, deseeded

1 jalapeño or other green chilli, deseeded

A good handful (40 g/1½ oz) of coriander, leaves and stems

Juice of 1 big lime

2 tbsp cider vinegar

7 tbsp extra virgin olive oil

300 ml/10 fl oz/1¼ cups water

Salt and pepper

TO SERVE
Diced avocado
Crushed tortilla chips

First transfer the cashews and their soaking liquid to a blender or food processor, then add the garlic and blitz until creamy. Add all the other ingredients and ½ teaspoon salt and some pepper and keep blitzing until you have a bright smooth soup. Adjust the seasoning to taste, you may want to add more vinegar or lime juice and maybe some more salt.

Chill in the fridge before serving in bowls topped with a little diced avocado and crushed tortilla chips.

WILD ROCKET & ROAST HAZELNUT PESTO

If you've been waiting for the summer season to make pesto, YOU'RE A FOOL, my friend. You can make pesto with all sorts of things, all year round. But I really love pairing peppery rocket with roasted hazelnuts to make a vibrant-green, deeply flavoured sauce. The key to this dish is to make sure you roast your hazelnuts to a nice and golden colour as this is where the flavour comes from.

Tip: Pesto is not just for pasta! You can stir it into your soup, spoon over grilled meat or fish, add sass to your sandwich, jazz up your veg or make a great salad with some fresh mozzarella and tomatoes.

Serves 4 (plus a little extra pesto for you to have during the week)

75 g/2¾ oz/½ cup blanched hazelnuts

1 big garlic clove, roughly chopped

180 g/6¼ oz wild rocket

200 ml/7 fl oz/1 cup olive oil, plus extra to serve

40 g/1½ oz/½ cup grated Parmesan cheese, plus extra to serve

350 g/12 oz dried spaghetti or penne

Salt and pepper

Preheat the oven to 170°C/150°C fan/250°F/gas mark 3. Spread the hazelnuts on a baking tray and roast for 10–12 minutes, allow to cool.

Bring a large pan of salted water to the boil and cook the pasta until al dente according to the packet instructions.

Place the nuts in a food processor (a blender is fine but a processor gives better texture) along with the garlic and ¾ tsp of salt. Blitz until you have breadcrumbs, then add the rocket and pulse-blitz until finely chopped. With the motor running, add the olive oil in a quick, steady stream. Transfer to a large bowl, stir in the cheese and check the seasoning.

Drain the cooked pasta, reserving a cupful of the cooking water. Add the pasta to the pesto bowl, stirring and tossing, adding a few tiny splashes of the water so you have a lovely, clingy sauce. Transfer to plates and sprinkle with a little extra Parmesan and some olive oil drizzled over.

PUMPKIN SOUP WITH SAGE & CHILLI OIL

Heaven in a bowl. The type of pumpkin/squash you use makes all the difference; I like to use an Italian Delica pumpkin, also known as Kabocha, which is super-flavoursome. Or, if you can get hold of a Crown Prince, that'd be great too. If not, butternut is good; I'd just go heavy on the herbs and chilli to give it a little help on its way.

Tip: Keep the pasta and soup separate if you're not planning on eating all in one go – nothing worse than leftover soup with soggy pasta! This is also great with spelt or pearl barley stirred through or cheesy **croûtons (p.152)**.

Serves 4

4 tbsp olive oil

1 onion, chopped

2 celery sticks, chopped

3 garlic cloves, chopped

600 g/1 lb 5 oz pumpkin or squash, peeled and cut into 15 mm/5-8in cubes

250 g/9 oz floury potatoes, such as Maris Piper, peeled and cut into 15 mm /5-8in cubes

1 x 225 g/8 oz can chopped tomatoes

1 tbsp thyme leaves

A few sprigs of rosemary leaves, picked and roughly chopped

200 g/7 oz/¾ cup small dried pasta, such as ditaloni or maccheroni

Salt and pepper

SAGE & CHILLI OIL

8 tbsp olive oil

8 sage leaves, roughly chopped

1 tbsp thyme leaves

½ tsp chilli flakes

In a deep pan over a medium-low heat, warm the oil and add the onion, celery, garlic and a big pinch of salt. Cover and cook, stirring occasionally, for 12–15 minutes until the veg is completely soft and sweet.

Add the pumpkin, potatoes, tomatoes and herbs to the pan.

Pour over 1.25 litres/2 pints/5½ cups of boiling water, add plenty of pepper and a couple of teaspoons of salt. Cover and leave to vigorously simmer for 20 minutes, stirring as often as you remember.

Meanwhile, bring a big pan of salted water to the boil and cook the pasta until al dente according to the packet instructions, then drain and rinse under cold running water to prevent it from sticking.

Next, make the sage and chilli oil. Place the oil, sage leaves, thyme leaves and chilli in a small pan over a low heat and cook for a few moments until you can see fine bubbles appear and it begins to simmer. Take off the heat and leave to infuse (it'll continue to simmer for a bit).

Once the pumpkin is tender, use a hand blender (or transfer to a blender) and blitz the soup until smoothish, though a few lumps are nice. Stir in the pasta, have a taste and adjust the seasoning.

Transfer to bowls and spoon over the sage and chilli oil before serving with some grated Parmesan, if you want.

TAKE
YOUR
TIME
WITH IT

TOMATO, TARRAGON & MUSTARD TART WITH CHEESY PUFF PASTRY

We can't have a lunch book without at least nodding to a quiche, can we? Small, sweet tomatoes are best for this as big ones can make this watery. The crisp, cheesy base is a fun trick and makes the tart taste like a giant cheese straw.

Tip: Pricking the pastry with a fork is quite important, otherwise the base puffs up and flings its topping around.

Serves 4

Flour, for dusting

425 g/15 oz not-too-ripe cherry or baby plum tomatoes, any colour

1 x 325 g/11½ oz pack ready-rolled puff pastry

150 g/5½ oz/1½ cups grated Gruyère, Gouda, mature Cheddar or Comté cheese, or a mix

3½ tbsp Dijon or wholegrain mustard

1½ tbsp crème fraîche, plus ½ tbsp extra for brushing

1 tbsp chopped tarragon or thyme leaves

Olive oil, for drizzling

Salt and pepper

Preheat the oven to 200°C/180°C fan/400°F/gas mark 6. Halve the tomatoes across the middle and press them, cut-side down, on some kitchen paper while you prepare everything else.

Open your pastry out onto a lightly floured surface. Roll it a little thinner, to make the rectangle about 35 x 24 cm/14 x 9½ in.

Scatter a large baking tray with a third of the grated cheese and sit the pastry on top. Score a 2 cm/1in border from the edge and prick the pastry all over with a fork. Place in the oven for 10 minutes, then allow to cool.

Meanwhile, mix the remaining cheese with the mustard, crème fraîche and herbs in a bowl. Spread within the border of the cooled pastry. Sit the tomatoes on top in a single layer, cut-side up, edges touching. Brush the border with a the extra crème fraîche, then drizzle the tomatoes with a little oil and season. Bake in the oven for 20 minutes until the pastry is golden and the tomatoes are very slightly coloured. This is delicious served warm or cool.

FALAFEL WITH SUMAC CHOP SALAD

You've not lived until you've made your own falafel; it'll transport you to Istanbul in one hot, herby mouthful. Please don't be put off by the long list of ingredients – most of them are thrown into the food processor anyway. And don't worry about getting all the salad ingredients, just use whatever you have/fancy, and chop 'em up into pea-sized pieces.

Tip: Just remember to soak the chickpeas the night before, this is the key to this recipe.

Serves 4

1 onion, roughly chopped

3 garlic cloves, roughly chopped

A small bunch of parsley or coriander, roughly chopped

½ small bunch of dill, roughly chopped

1 tsp ground cumin

1 tsp ground coriander

300 g/10½ oz/1½ cups dried chickpeas, soaked overnight in cold water

3 tbsp gram flour

2 tsp baking powder

Sunflower oil, for frying

SUMAC CHOP SALAD

1 cucumber, chopped into cubes

2 handfuls of radishes, quartered

1 Little Gem lettuce, chopped

1 large tomato, chopped

Seeds from ½ small pomegranate

2 tbsp olive oil

3 tsp sumac

Juice of 1 lemon

Salt and pepper

1 batch of **tahini sauce (p.139)**, to serve

Put the onion, garlic, herbs and spices in a food processor and blitz until coarsely chopped.

Drain the soaked chickpeas, and roughly dry them in a clean tea towel. Add to the processor along with ½ teaspoon salt, the flour and baking powder and blitz again until everything is finely chopped.

Transfer to a mixing bowl. You should be able to grab a handful of the mix and it will hold together. If not, add more flour. Pop in the fridge while you make the salad.

Chuck the salad ingredients into a bowl, drizzle in the oil and sprinkle in the sumac. Don't toss yet or add the lemon juice and seasoning – hold off until just before eating so everything stays crunchy. Put to one side.

Meanwhile, make the tahini sauce and put to one side. Line a plate or tray with kitchen paper. Pour some vegetable oil into a heavy-based pan, ideally a wok, and add enough oil to come 5–6 cm 2–2½in in up the sides. Put over a medium-high heat and heat until it registers 160–180°C/320–350°F on a jam thermometer or until a small chunk of bread sizzles and turns golden in 30 seconds. Using 2 tablespoons, shape 1 tablespoonful of the falafel mix into an oval-shaped ball and very carefully slide into the hot oil. This makes approximately 20-24 falafels. Keep going until all your mix is cooking but don't overcrowd the pan (do this in batches if necessary). Cook the falafel for 2 minutes, then roll over to cook the other side for a further 2 minutes. Scoop them out once dark golden and crisp, and drain on the kitchen paper. Break open one to check that the inside is nicely cooked. If not, your oil may be a little too hot.

Squeeze the lemon over the salad, season and toss. Serve the falafel immediately with lots of tahini sauce and some flatbreads. Also delicious with the **roast beet & cumin hummus (p.141)**.

KOFTE WITH SPICED TOMATO, GARLIC YOGURT & HERBS

Serves 4

SPICED TOMATO SAUCE

3 tbsp olive oil

2 garlic cloves, sliced

2 x 400 g/14 oz cans chopped tomatoes or 800 g/1 lb 12 oz/4 cups passata

½ tsp ground cinnamon

Salt and pepper

KOFTE

1 tbsp ground cumin

1 tbsp ground coriander

2 garlic cloves, finely chopped

600 g/1 lb 5 oz lamb or beef mince

2 tsp Pul biber or 1 red chilli, finely chopped

GARLIC YOGURT

1 small garlic clove, peeled

150 g/5½ oz/ ½ cup Greek yogurt

HERBY SALAD

4 handfuls of parsley leaves

4 handfuls of rocket

A large handful of mint leaves

2 tsp sumac or juice of ½ lemon

1 tbsp olive oil

When grilled meat meets spiced tomato sauce and they're joined by garlic yogurt, beautiful things happen. Cook this and you'll agree with me.

Tip: Don't forget to soak 4 wooden skewers in cold water for 30 minutes if you're barbecuing these.

Get the tomato sauce going first. Warm the olive oil in a wide frying pan over a medium heat and gently fry the garlic until it becomes sticky and coloured on the edges, about 2-3 minutes. Add the tomatoes, cinnamon and some seasoning and leave the sauce to simmer vigorously for at least 15 minutes while you prepare everything else. You may need to add a little water if it begins to look a little dry.

Transfer all the kofte ingredients to a bowl, season well and combine with your hands. Divide into four and roll each piece into a sausage shape before pushing a skewer through the middle. Place in the fridge if you have time.

Make the garlic yogurt by finely grating the garlic into the yogurt, then season lightly.

Combine all the herby salad ingredients in a bowl, season lightly and put to one side.

Heat a griddle pan, frying pan or barbecue until hot and grill the kofte for 5–7 minutes until cooked, turning them as soon as each side has char marks. Leave to rest for a few minutes.

Sit the cooked kofte on top of the tomato sauce and serve with dollops of the garlic yogurt, the herby salad and warm **flatbreads (p.155)** to scoop it up with.

Take Your Time with it

CHICKEN SHAWARMA WITH GREEN TAHINI CHICKPEA SALAD

Serves 4

1 tbsp ground coriander

1 tbsp ground cumin

1 tsp Turkish pepper flakes (pul biber) or ½ tsp cayenne pepper, plus (optional) extra to serve

1 tsp sweet paprika

Juice of ½ lemon

3 tbsp olive oil

4 large skin-on, bone-in chicken thighs, at room temp

Salt and pepper

CHICKPEA SALAD

½ red onion, finely sliced

Juice of 1 lemon, plus extra for wedges to serve

½ tsp caster sugar

1 small garlic clove, roughly chopped

3 tbsp tahini

2 tbsp olive oil

A large handful of flat-leaf parsley

A small handful of mint leaves

2 x 400 g/14 oz cans chickpeas, drained and rinsed

3 big handfuls of ripe cherry tomatoes, halved

1 cucumber, halved lengthways, seeds discarded, chopped

This is my version of that famous kebab shop dish that we all secretly love but treat like a shameful secret. But this is quicker, easier and healthier. AND no rotating vertical spit or extra long break knife needed.

Tip: The chicken would definitely benefit from an overnight marinade, if you have time. I'd add a few crushed cloves of garlic too.

Preheat the oven to 220°C/200°C fan/425°F/gas mark 7. Combine all the spices, lemon juice, oil and ½ teaspoon of salt in a bowl, add the thighs and rub the mix into them so they're nicely coated. Place them, skin-side up, in a large baking tin (make sure there's some space between them) and cook in the oven for 25–30 minutes until the skin is crisp and the juices run clear.

Meanwhile, make the salad. Put the onion in a small bowl, squeeze over half the lemon and sprinkle with the sugar and a pinch of salt. Put to one side to pickle.

Put the chopped garlic, tahini, oil, most of the herbs, the juice from the remaining ½ lemon and 3 tablespoons of water in a mini food processor or blender and blitz until you have a fluffy, vibrant green dressing the texture of whipped cream. Season to taste.

Put the chickpeas, tomatoes, cucumber and pickled onion and its liquid in a salad bowl and pour over the tahini dressing. Taste and add some seasoning and a little more lemon juice, if you wish.

Rest the chicken for 5 minutes, then transfer to plates, spoon over any lovely roasting juices and serve with the salad, sprinkled with the remaining herbs and extra pepper flakes, if you wish.

Take Your Time with it

SWEET POTATO, BLACK BEAN & CHIMICHURRI TACOS

Serves 4   (VE)

4 tbsp olive oil

2 tsp sweet paprika

750 g/1 lb 10 oz sweet potatoes, scrubbed, quartered lengthways and cut into 2.5cm/1in thick chunks

Salt and pepper

BLACK BEANS

2½ tbsp olive oil

1 garlic clove, sliced

1 tsp cumin seeds

1 x 400 g/14 oz can black beans, drained and rinsed

CHIMICHURRI

1 small garlic clove, roughly chopped

1 red chilli, roughly chopped

A big bunch of coriander, leaves and stalks, roughly chopped

½ tsp cumin seeds

2 tbsp red wine vinegar

100 ml/3½ fl oz/½ cup olive oil

½ red onion, finely chopped

TO SERVE

12 small corn or flour tortillas

½ small red or white cabbage, shredded

Juice of ½–1 lime

Quick pickled onions (p.146)

These are my go-to quick tacos when I'm not in a meat mood – the contrast of sweet, caramel-y potato and sassy, spicy chimichurri makes for serious fireworks in your mouth. It's a combination of ingredients that tickles all those taste buds. These would be sensational with some **quick pickled onions (p.146)** on top.

Tip: Wrap the tortillas in foil in stacks of 6 and put in the oven below the sweet potatoes (or feel free to warm in a pan, if you like).

Preheat the oven to 220°C/200°C fan/425°F/gas mark 7. Line a large baking tray with greaseproof paper. Toss together the 4 tablespoons of oil, the paprika and some seasoning in a bowl, then chuck in the sweet potatoes and toss well so they're nicely coated. Spread out on the baking tray and roast for 20–25 minutes, stirring once, until crisp on the edges but tender inside.

Make the black beans. Warm the oil in a small pan over a medium heat and fry the garlic and a pinch of salt for 2–3 minutes until the garlic is beginning to colour. Add the cumin seeds, wait a second for them to warm through, then add the black beans, 50ml/2 fl oz/¼ cup of water to just cover them, and a big pinch of salt. Simmer for 10 minutes until the water has reduced while you make the chimichurri.

To make the chimichurri, throw everything except the vinegar, oil and red onion into your food processor or blender and pulse-blitz until roughly chopped (you can also do this by hand). Add the vinegar, oil and ½ tablespoon of water and blitz until you have a finely chopped green sauce. Transfer to a small bowl and stir in the chopped onion. Season with salt so it tastes lively. Warm the tortillas (see tip above).

Finally, toss the cabbage in the lime juice and a little salt. Have a taste and add more lime, if you wish.

When everything is ready, divide the beans between the tortillas and add a small handful of cabbage. Sit the sweet potatoes on top, spoon over the chimichurri and eat immediately. Alternatively, I like to serve everything in bowls for everyone to help themselves.

WARM FARRO WITH CAVOLO NERO PESTO & RICOTTA

This is based on the technique for the exceptionally delicious **super greens sauce (p.72)** but it uses farro instead of pasta. I make it regularly in the colder months when cavolo is at its best and this kind of wholesome comfort food is exactly what the weather calls for.

Tip: Any leftovers will taste great the next day for a lunchbox and will reheat (and freeze) happily.

Serves 4

250 g/9 oz/1 cup farro, pearled spelt or pearled barley, rinsed

105 ml/3½ fl oz/½ cup olive oil

1 onion, chopped

3 small garlic cloves, 2 whole and peeled, 1 chopped

A pinch of chilli flakes, optional

400 g/14 oz cavolo nero/or Savoy cabbage (or a mix), stripped of stems

75 g/2¾ oz/¾ cups grated Parmesan cheese, plus extra to serve

6 tbsp ricotta

Salt and pepper

Bring a large pan of salted water to the boil and cook the farro for 20–25 minutes until tender, following the packet instructions, then drain.

Meanwhile, warm 2 tablespoons of the olive oil in a large frying pan over a medium heat and fry the onion, the 1 chopped garlic clove, the chilli and a big pinch of salt until soft, about 10–12 minutes. Chop 2 handfuls of the cavolo (ideally damp from washing) and add that to the pan too, cooking for 5–7 minutes until soft.

Bring another big pan of salted water to the boil. Add the remaining cavolo and the 2 whole garlic cloves and cook for 5–6 minutes until just tender, then drain, keeping a cupful of the cooking water. Transfer the cooked cavolo and garlic to a blender (or use a hand blender) and blitz with the remaining 75 ml/2½fl oz/5 tbsp of olive oil, the Parmesan and the reserved cooking water. Add a good grinding of black pepper and blitz to a purée, adding a few more splashes of cooking water to give the consistency of double cream, if needed.

Stir the cooked farro into the fried onion mix, then pour in the cavolo sauce. Simmer for 3 minutes so the farro absorbs the sauce, adding more water if it looks a little dry. Transfer to plates and spoon over a little ricotta, a good extra dusting of Parmesan and a little extra oil before serving.

Take Your Time with it

CHANA MASALA

I discovered this recipe through my friend Stevie Parle and probably make it every two weeks. It's moreish, incredibly satisfying and full of Indian spices that all get sucked up by the chickpeas. A perfect lunch on its own with a spoonful of yogurt, Indian breads and pickles or chutneys. You want everything lined up and ready to go, a bit like making a stir-fry.

Tip: I'd recommend doubling the recipe and getting the leftovers in the freezer for when you don't have the energy to cook but need something wholesome.

Serves 4

3 tbsp olive oil

1 heaped tsp cumin seeds

2 tsp coriander seeds, lightly crushed

½ tsp ground turmeric

½ tsp chilli flakes

1 small onion, finely chopped

2 garlic cloves, finely chopped

A small thumb of ginger, peeled and finely chopped

A big bunch of coriander, stalks finely chopped, leaves roughly chopped

2 x 400 g/14 oz cans plum tomatoes, drained and rinsed

2 x 400 g/14 oz cans chickpeas, drained and rinsed

Juice of ½–1 lime

Salt and pepper

TO SERVE
Natural yogurt
Chapattis, rotis or naan
Indian pickles or chutneys

Warm the olive oil in a large saucepan over a low heat. When warm, add the cumin seeds and, after 5 seconds or so, add all the remaining spices and allow them to warm through for just a moment before adding the onion, garlic, ginger and chopped coriander stalks – the leaves get added later.

Turn up the heat to medium, add a big pinch of salt and leave to cook for 8–10 minutes until the onion is completely soft. Add the tomatoes, breaking them up with a spoon, then add the chickpeas and 150 ml/5 fl oz/⅔ cup of water. Season well, bring to the boil, then lower the heat and leave to simmer without a lid for another 15 minutes.

To finish, taste and adjust the seasoning, then squeeze in the half lime (adding more, if you like) and stir in the coriander leaves so they just wilt. Serve immediately with yogurt, chapattis and Indian pickles/chutneys.

SWEET & SPICY SILKEN TOFU WITH STICKY JASMINE RICE

For me this dish is comfort food that's had a flavour bomb thrown at it. But the best thing? No cooking skills needed here it's so perfect for some automatic cooking on those tired days when you need a plate of delicious food without any challenges.

Zha cai is a type of preserved pickled vegetable that you can find in little foil sachets in Chinese supermarkets. I'm obsessed with its chewy/crunchy texture and sweet-sour flavour. Kimchi would be a very fine substitute (though I'd reduce the chilli oil) as would kraut or even some chopped pickled cucumber.

Serves 4

350 g/12 oz/1½ cups jasmine rice, rinsed

600 g/1 lb 5 oz silken tofu

6 tbsp light soy sauce, or to taste

2½ tbsp chilli oil, such as Chiu Chow, plus extra to serve

2 tbsp sesame oil

2 tbsp rice wine vinegar

3 tsp caster sugar

60 g/2¼ oz/½ cup zha cai or kimchi, roughly chopped

6 spring onions, thinly sliced

Salt

TO SERVE, OPTIONAL
Crispy fried onions
Coriander, roughly chopped
Steamed spinach

Bring 600ml/1 pint/2 ½ cups of water to the boil. Tip the rice into the measured water, cover, and turn down to a simmer for 15-18 minutes. Briefly remove the lid to check it's done (add a drop more water and keep cooking if not) and return the lid to rest while you prepare everything else.

For the tofu, bring a separate pan of water to the boil and add ½ teaspoon of salt. Carefully remove the tofu from its packet, trying to not break it up too much, then lower into the water and simmer for 5 minutes, don't worry if it breaks up a little.

Meanwhile, combine the soy, chilli oil, sesame oil, vinegar and sugar in a bowl, stirring until the sugar dissolves. Stir in the zha cai and spring onions and put to one side for a moment.

Carefully drain the tofu into a sieve. Fluff up the rice with a fork, then divide between bowls, and while the tofu is still nice and hot, scoop tablespoonfuls onto the rice. Spoon the sauce over the top and eat immediately with a little extra chilli oil and, if you wish, some crispy fried onions, chopped coriander and steamed spinach.

MELTY MEATBALL
& MOZZARELLA SUB

Just in case you've spent your whole life eating your meatballs with spaghetti... you need to join the meatballs-in-your-sandwich-club immediately.

Tip: If you have some herbs, such as parsley, thyme, sage or rosemary in your fridge, throw them into your meatballs too.

Makes 4

TOMATO SAUCE

3 tbsp olive oil

2 garlic cloves, sliced

2 x 400 g/14 oz cans chopped tomatoes or 800g/1 lb 12 oz/4 cups passata

Salt and pepper

MEATBALLS

100 g/3½ oz/2 cups fresh breadcrumbs, soaked in 4 tbsp water

400 g/14 oz pork or beef mince (or a mix)

2 eggs, beaten

1 garlic clove, crushed with a little salt

1 tbsp fennel seeds

50 g/1¾ oz/⅓ cups grated Parmesan cheese

A pinch of chilli flakes

TO SERVE

1 large baguette, split lengthways and cut across into 4 equal pieces

A small handful of basil leaves, optional

200 g/7 oz fresh mozzarella or scamorza, drained on kitchen paper and roughly torn or grated

Preheat the oven to 220°C/200°C fan/425°F/gas mark 7.

Begin with the tomato sauce. Warm the olive oil in a wide pan or frying pan over a medium heat and gently fry the garlic until it becomes sticky and coloured on the edges, about 2-3 minutes. Add the tomatoes and some seasoning and leave the sauce to simmer vigorously for at least 20-25 minutes while you get on with everything else.

Meanwhile, put all the meatball ingredients in a bowl, add a generous amount of seasoning and scrunch everything together with your hands. Shape into 21 golf balls (includes one for you to check!), about 40 g/1½ oz each. Place on a greased baking tray and pop in the oven for 8–10 minutes until coloured all over but still with some give when squeezed. Check one in the middle, it should be just cooked and nice and moist. Keep the oven on but turn to the grill setting.

Make sure the tomato sauce is simmering and that it's not too dry – you may want to add a splash of water so that it can nicely coat the meatballs. Add the meatballs to the sauce, turn them gently in the sauce and simmer for another 2–3 minutes; by this time they should feel a little firmer when squeezed.

Arrange the bottom half of the baguette portions on the meatball baking tray. Spoon some of the tomato sauce over the pieces so the bread can soak it in and top with the meatballs and remaining sauce. Sprinkle over the mozzarella and pop under the grill until the cheese is melted and delicious. Rip over the basil (if using), add the baguette tops and GO FOR IT!

Take Your Time with it

SESAME CHICKEN SCHNITZEL WITH KIMCHI COLESLAW

This way of making schnitzel with fresh bread is very clever (thank you, Jamie Oliver). They crisp up beautifully and give it an amazing, soft-on-the-inside, crisp-on-the-outside texture. It's also slightly less messy than the egg/flour/crumbs technique. The slaw is possibly one of the most addictive things you can put in your mouth and exactly what you want with a schnitzel: a little bit sour and a little bit spicy. I challenge you not to start putting it on everything.

Serves 4

4 boneless, skinless large chicken thigh or small chicken breasts

300 g/10½ oz seeded wholemeal bread slices, crusts removed

4 tbsp sesame seeds

Sunflower oil, for frying

COLESLAW

75 g/2¾ oz/⅔ cup kimchi, plus 1 tbsp of its brine

1 tsp fish sauce

Juice of 1 lime

2 tsp sesame oil

3 tbsp olive oil

1½ tsp caster sugar

½ head of Chinese cabbage or 1 white cabbage, finely shredded

4 spring onions, finely sliced

2 carrots, julienned (or make ribbons with a regular peeler)

Salt and pepper

TO SERVE

Sriracha

Kimchi

Lime wedges

If using chicken breasts, sit them cut-side up on a chopping board, and slice into them horizontally, about three-quarters of the way through to open them up like a book (skip this step if using thighs). One at a time, place the chicken thighs or breasts between a folded sheet of greased greaseproof paper. Use a heavy object like a rolling pin or frying pan to bash and evenly flatten the schnitzels to about 5 mm/¼in thick. Try to avoid breaking them, but it's not a disaster if you do.

Tear the bread into pieces and put in a food processor. Blitz until you have fine breadcrumbs. Stir in the sesame seeds.

Sit a flattened piece of chicken on one side of the greaseproof paper and sprinkle generously with the sesame breadcrumbs, pressing the crumbs into the chicken. Cover with the other half of the paper and bash again with the rolling pin to hammer the crumbs into the chicken, then turn it over to coat the other side, in the same way. Repeat this process until all the chicken is nicely covered. Put on a plate in the fridge while you prepare the coleslaw.

Put the kimchi, fish sauce, lime juice, the oils and the sugar in a small blender and blitz until smooth. Season to taste. Tip the cabbage, spring onions and carrots into a large bowl, pour over the dressing and combine with your hands. Set to one side while you cook the chicken.

Turn on your oven to low to keep the chicken warm. Set a large, heavy-based frying pan over a medium heat and pour in enough oil to come 1 cm/½in up the sides. Get the oil hot enough to brown a breadcrumb in 10 seconds, and then lower in two schnitzels (depending on your pan size) and cook until golden brown, about 2–3 minutes on each side. Transfer to the warm oven while you cook the other pieces, scooping out any large breadcrumbs that look to be burning, then serve.

Allow the schnitzels to rest for a minute or so, then transfer to plates. Pile the coleslaw next to the chicken and serve with a little extra kimchi, if you like.

EGGS IN MEXICAN PURGATORY WITH CHIPOTLE CREMA

There are a million different versions of eggs baked in tomato sauce, but I love the ones with Mexican spicing. The contrast of the tangy chipotle crema really brings this to life.

Tip: Adjust the amounts of chipotles in adobo paste according to your taste (see p.26 for a cheat's version). Canned tomatoes are fine, you may just want to cook them for a bit longer to sweeten them.

Serves 2-4

3 tbsp olive oil

1 onion, finely chopped

2 garlic cloves, finely chopped

1 tsp ground cumin

½ tsp ground cinnamon

1 tsp sweet paprika

1-2 tbsp chipotles in adobo paste, depending on their strength

750 g/1 lb 10 oz fresh tomatoes, cut into small chunks

½ tbsp soft light brown sugar

1 tbsp red wine vinegar

4 eggs

Salt and pepper

CHIPOTLE CREMA

½ garlic clove, peeled

100 g /3½ oz/½ cup Greek or natural yogurt

1-2 tsp chipotles in adobo paste, depending on their strength

1 tsp ketchup

Juice of ½ small lime

TO SERVE

1-2 ripe avocados, stoned, peeled and sliced

A handful of coriander leaves

Tortillas or toast

Preheat the oven to 200°C/180°C fan/400°F/gas mark 6. Warm the olive oil in a large, ovenproof frying pan (or you can cook in the saucepan and transfer to a baking dish later) over a medium heat, add the onion and a big pinch of salt and gently fry for 8–10 minutes until soft, adding the garlic for the final 2 minutes.

Add the spices, cook for another 15 seconds, then add the chipotles, tomatoes, sugar and vinegar and another big pinch of salt. Simmer for 5–10 minutes so all the flavours are mingling. Have a taste and adjust the seasoning if needed.

While the sauce is simmering, make the chipotle crema. Grate the garlic straight into the yogurt, then stir in all the other ingredients and season to taste. Put to one side for a moment.

With a wooden spoon, make small indents in the sauce and crack in the eggs. Transfer to the oven for 10–12 minutes until the whites are just set but the yolks are still runny.

When you're ready to eat, serve the eggs garnished with avocado slices, a few coriander leaves and a big drizzle of the chipotle crema. Warm tortillas or make toast – essential to scoop up all the juiciness.

WILD GARLIC GREEN BAKED EGGS

This is super-fresh, but a little bit decadent too. Exactly how I like my eggs. Wilting wild garlic softens its punch and brings out the sweetness so it ends up tasting a bit like its pal, spinach. If you have extra wild garlic, very finely chop it and stir through some soft butter (about 15 g/½ oz of wild garlic per 150 g/5½ oz/¾ cup of butter) to make a very sexy wild garlic butter which you can smother on toast, stuff into a chicken kiev, put into a baked potato.... However, if you can't get hold of wild garlic, use extra spinach and combine with some chopped garlic fried in oil.

Serves 2

30 g/1 oz wild garlic leaves,
   washed
200 g/7 oz fresh spinach or
   150 g/5½ oz frozen spinach
4 tbsp crème fraîche or soured
   cream
5 tbsp grated Parmesan cheese
4 eggs
Olive oil, for drizzling
Salt and pepper
Garlic-rubbed buttery toast

Preheat the oven to 200°C/180°C fan/400°F/gas mark 6.

Wilt the wild garlic and spinach in a large, dry, ovenproof frying pan (or you can cook the sauce in a saucepan and transfer to a baking dish later) with a splash of water over a medium heat. Stir in a few pinches of salt, followed by the crème fraîche and 4 tablespoons of the Parmesan. Stir until the crème fraîche and Parmesan have melted, then add a little more water to make a wet sauce. Season to taste.

Make small indents in the sauce and crack in the eggs. Sprinkle with the remaining tablespoon of Parmesan and drizzle over a little oil. Bake for 10–12 minutes until the whites are just set but the yolks are still runny. Eat immediately with garlic-rubbed buttery toast.

BATTERED PRAWN TACOS WITH CHIPOTLE MAYO & MANGO SLAW

Serves 4

12 small flour tortillas

Sunflower oil, for frying

300 g/10½ oz/2 cups raw peeled king prawns

1 lime, quartered, to serve

MANGO SLAW

1 small, not-too-ripe mango, peeled, stoned and sliced into matchsticks

½ red onion, finely sliced

100 g/3½ oz/1 cup red cabbage, finely sliced

75 g/2¾ oz/⅔ cup radishes, finely sliced

2 handfuls of coriander leaves

8 cherry tomatoes, quartered

Juice of 1 lime, plus extra, to serve

Salt

CHIPOTLE MAYO

150 g/5½ oz mayonnaise shop-bought or **homemade (p.142)** or soured cream

3–4 tsp chipotles in adobo paste, depending on their strength

2 tsp ketchup

BATTER

100 g/3½ oz/¾ cup plain flour

½ tsp bicarbonate of soda

185 ml/6½ fl oz/¾ cup cold Corona or other beer

2–4 tbsp iced water

This dish is a riot of colours and will take you straight to the sunny beaches of Baja. It's easier than it looks too. You can prepare everything in advance and just do a bit of deep-frying before serving. Make sure you're drinking the rest of that beer while you're cooking this, please.

Prepare the slaw first by combining the mango, onion, cabbage, radishes, coriander and tomatoes in a mixing bowl. Dress with the lime juice and some salt and pop in the fridge to stay crisp while you get everything else ready.

Make the chipotle mayo next by stirring the mayo, chipotles and ketchup together in a small bowl. Set aside.

When you're ready to eat, make the batter. Put the flour, bicarbonate and ½ teaspoon of salt in a mixing bowl and whisk in the beer and iced water, starting with 2 tablespoons and seeing if you need more. Stir until just mixed. You want the batter to be the consistency of double cream. A few lumps are fine; try to avoid over-mixing.

Warm your tortillas next so they're ready for you. Either wrap them in foil in stacks of 6 and warm in a hot oven, or put a frying pan over a medium-high heat and once hot, dry-fry each tortilla, wrapping them in a clean tea towel to keep warm as you go.

In a deep, heavy-based pan or wok, heat up enough sunflower oil so that it comes 5–6 cm/2–2½ in up the sides of the pan. Put over a medium-high heat and heat until it registers 160–180°C/320–350°F on a jam thermometer or until a small chunk of bread sizzles and turns golden in 30 seconds. Line a plate with kitchen paper to drain the prawns and have a slotted spoon at hand.

Dip the prawns in the batter to coat on all sides, then very carefully lower them, one at a time, into the hot oil, cooking them in batches so they're not crowded. Allow the oil to return to temperature after each batch. Remove each prawn with the slotted spoon once deep golden – about 45 seconds–1 minute. Drain on the kitchen paper as you fry the rest.

To assemble the tacos, pile some slaw into the warm tortillas then add a couple or so battered prawns on top and dollop a tablespoonful of chipotle mayo on top. Serve with lime wedges for squeezing.

VIETNAMESE STICKY TOFU BUN CHA

This is such a great one for lunch as it's full of variety but isn't too heavy, so you can continue to fly through your day. It's brilliant cold too so if you want to pack it up, use a few handfuls of finely shredded cabbage instead of Little Gem and it will stay crunchier for longer.

Tip: A julienne peeler is a great investment for your utensil collection. They cost the same as a normal peeler and will upgrade your coleslaws to first class

Serves 4

150 g/5½ oz dried rice vermicelli or glass noodles

1 tbsp sesame oil

2 carrots, peeled and julienned (see **Tip**)

2 Little Gem or 1 Romaine lettuce, finely shredded

4 spring onions, finely sliced

A small bunch of coriander or Thai basil, roughly chopped

2 handfuls of mint leaves, roughly chopped

DRESSING

2 tsp soft light brown sugar

1 garlic clove, grated

1 red chilli, deseeded and chopped

3 tbsp light soy sauce

3 tbsp rice wine vinegar

1 tbsp sesame oil

Juice of 1 lime

TOFU

600 g/1 lb 5 oz firm tofu, drained

2 tbsp sunflower oil

6 tbsp hoisin sauce

1 tbsp light soy sauce

40 g/1½ oz/½ cup roasted salted peanuts, chopped, to serve

First wrap the tofu in a clean tea towel or sheets of kitchen paper. Place between two chopping boards and put a saucepan or a few unopened cans on top to help press out the water. Leave like this while you prepare everything else.

Cook the noodles following the packet instructions. Be careful not to overcook them: a little al dente is preferable. Drain and rinse under cold running water until cool, then toss in the sesame oil and put to one side.

Combine the carrots, lettuce, spring onions and herbs in a bowl.

Stir all the dressing ingredients together until the sugar dissolves, then spoon over the salad and toss well. Keep in the fridge while you cook the tofu.

Unwrap the tofu and cut it into 3 cm/1¼in chunks. Heat the sunflower oil in a large frying pan over a medium-high heat, then add the tofu and fry for about 5–6 minutes, turning as each side turns golden. The more sides you brown, the crispier it will be, but it's fine to only do a couple of sides if you want to hurry through.

Mix the hoisin and soy sauces, then add to the pan and turn the tofu in the sauce until everything is coated and sticky. Take off the heat after a minute or so. Divide the noodles between plates, top with the salad, followed by the sticky fried tofu, then spoon over the dressing and serve scattered with the peanuts.

Take Your Time with it

RED LENTIL COCONUT DAHL

Serves 4

300 g/10½ oz/1½ cups dried red
  lentils, rinsed

3 tbsp olive or coconut oil

2 large red onions, chopped –
  reserve 4 tbsp for the sambol

3 garlic cloves, chopped

2 green chillies, chopped –
  reserve 1 chopped chilli for
  the sambol

2 tsp garam masala

1½ tsp ground cumin

1½ tsp ground turmeric

1 tsp ground coriander

3 tomatoes, roughly chopped

1 x 400 g/14 oz can coconut milk

Salt and pepper

COCONUT SAMBOL

4 tbsp red onion, chopped (see
  above)

1 green chilli, chopped (see
  above)

A pinch of chilli flakes

50 g/1¾ oz/½ cup desiccated
  coconut

Zest and juice of 1 lime

SERVING SUGGESTIONS

Bombay or Bhel Puri mix

Mango chutney

Lime pickle

Garlic yogurt (½ grated garlic
  clove stirred into 75 g/2¾
  oz/¼ cup coconut yogurt)

A handful of fresh coriander
  leaves

Five-minute fluffy flatbreads
  (p.155)

I live for this stuff. It is everything you could want in a plate of food: filling, comforting, full of delicious, warming flavours AND – the best bit – incredibly healthy and nutritious. The sambol is super-quick and easy to whip up; just chop extra onions and chilli when you're making the dahl and put them to one side. It gives this dish an extra pop, making every mouthful different.

Tip: Freeze any leftovers so you can always have this waiting for you.

Put the lentils in a pan with ½ teaspoon of salt and cover with plenty of cold water. Bring to the boil (skimming off any scum that rises), then reduce to a simmer and cook gently for 15–20 minutes until completely tender, topping up the water if needed. Once the lentils are cooked, add (or drain) some water for your desired consistency – you want to aim for porridge.

Meanwhile, warm the oil in a large frying pan, add the onions with a big pinch of salt, and fry for 5–7 minutes until they are turning translucent, then add the garlic and chilli and cook for a further 5 minutes until everything is soft and sweet. Stir in the spices and fry for a minute or two, then add the chopped tomatoes and season generously with salt. Leave to simmer while the lentils finish cooking.

Meanwhile, make the sambol. Combine the reserved chopped onion and chilli with the chilli flakes, coconut and lime zest and juice and season generously with salt and pepper. Scrunch together with your hands so everything gets really mixed in, then put to one side.

Stir the lentils and the coconut milk into the tomato mix, return to the boil and cook for a couple of minutes until everything is nicely hanging out together. Taste and adjust the seasoning. Spoon into bowls or plates, top with a big spoonful of the sambol, plus any of the serving suggestions.

Take Your Time with it

PRUNE & PORK GIANT SAUSAGE ROLLS WITH MUSTARDY CHICORY SALAD

I don't think these need selling to you. I'll just say ... these are best straight from the oven when the pastry is at peak deliciousness (but they are very happy to be reheated briefly too).

Tip: Use your pastry straight from the fridge and try not to faff with it too much as your rolls will lose their shape in the oven.

Serves 4

Sunflower oil, for greasing

400 g/14 oz good-quality sausage meat (or 8 nice sausages, skins discarded)

70 g/2½ oz/1 cup stoned dried prunes, finely chopped

1 tbsp finely chopped sage

1½ tsp fennel seeds

1 x 320 g/11½ oz pack ready-rolled puff pastry

1 egg, beaten with a splash of milk

1 tbsp sesame seeds

Pepper

MUSTARDY CHICORY SALAD

½ batch of **creamy mustard dressing (p.149)**

4 heads of red and/or white chicory or radicchio, leaves halved lengthways

8 radishes, halved

A handful of parsley leaves

1 tbsp capers, soaked if salted

Preheat the oven to 220°C/200°C fan/425°F/gas mark 7 and grease a baking tray with oil.

Put the sausage meat in a bowl with the prunes, sage and fennel seeds, grind in some pepper and combine with your hands until just mixed. Don't overdo it though as you don't want to melt the fat in the meat too much.

Open your pastry out onto a baking tray lined with greaseproof paper (or use what the pastry is rolled in). Shape the meat into a long sausage (roughly the length of the pastry) and place along one long side of the pastry, leaving a 4 cm/1½in border. Brush the edge with some of the beaten egg, then fold over the other side and gently squeeze to seal around the sausage meat. Slice away any excess pastry, leaving a 2 cm/¾in border. Seal with the prongs of a fork. Cut into 4 even pieces and separate them on the paper.

Brush the top of each roll with more beaten egg, sprinkle with the sesame seeds and bake for 20 minutes or until golden all over.

While they cook, mix the mustard dressing in the bottom of a salad bowl and add the rest of the ingredients on top. As soon as the sausage rolls come out of the oven, toss the salad and serve alongside the warm sausage rolls with a little extra mustard if you're that way inclined.

4 FRITTATAS

COURGETTE, SPINACH & RICOTTA FRITTATA

Courgette flowers add an extra pretty *je ne sais quoi*, but I appreciate they're not the easiest things to get your hands on. This tastes great, with or without the flowers.

Serves 4

3 tbsp olive oil

A bunch of spring onions, sliced

1 garlic clove, finely chopped

4 courgettes, grated on the finest side of a box grater

200 g/7 oz/1¼ cups fresh spinach, chopped

8 eggs, beaten

200 g/7 oz/1 cup ricotta

80 g/3 oz/¾ cup grated Parmesan cheese

4 courgette flowers, optional, ripped into quarters

Salt and pepper

Preheat the grill to high. Warm the oil in a wide, ovenproof frying pan over a medium heat. Add the spring onions, garlic and a big pinch of salt and fry for 2–3 minutes until the onions are soft.

Turn the heat up a bit and add the grated courgettes and stir once. Leave them undisturbed for 3 minutes or so to get a little colour, then stir and keep cooking until you can see they're softened. Stir in the chopped spinach, folding it into the courgette mixture until it has wilted and is nicely combined.

Season the eggs, then pour over the courgettes. Cook gently for 3–4 minutes until you can see that the bottom is firm (the top will still be runny).

Combine the ricotta with half the Parmesan and season lightly. Once you've got a firm bottom on your eggs, dollop over the ricotta, pushing it gently under the still-runny eggs. Arrange your flowers on top (if using) and sprinkle over the rest of the Parmesan. Put under the grill for 4–5 minutes until the cheese is melted and the frittata is just cooked in the middle (though a little soft and runny is no bad thing). Allow to rest for 5 minutes, then transfer to a large plate if you can or serve straight from the pan.

'NDUJA, MASCARPONE & SPAGHETTI FRITTATA

If you've ever worked in an Italian restaurant, it's very likely you've been served this for staff food. Like most people, I was initially a little suspicious of it, then completely charmed. It's a brilliant way to use up leftover spaghetti, especially if it's already in its sauce. Just add cheese and whatever bits you have lying around, such as peas, greens, herbs. Here I'm using plain spaghetti and 'nduja for its speedy flavour injection.

Serves 4

1 tbsp olive oil

25 g/1 oz 'nduja

125 g/4½ oz/¾ cup mascarpone

300 g/10½ oz cooked spaghetti
(or whatever leftovers you
have) (150 g /5½ oz raw
weight)

80 g/3 oz/¾ cup mature
Cheddar or Parmesan
cheese, grated

8 eggs, beaten

Salt and pepper

Preheat the grill to high. Warm the oil in a wide, ovenproof frying pan over a medium heat and add 20 g/¾ oz of the 'nduja. Fry for a moment until it melts into a red oil, then stir in three-quarters of the mascarpone and half the cheese, squishing them into the 'nduja to make a vibrant orange sauce.

Stir in the spaghetti and toss until every strand is covered in sauce. Lightly season the eggs, then pour over the spaghetti. Stir briefly to incorporate everything, then cook gently for 3–4 minutes until you can see that the bottom is firm (the top will still be runny).

Once you've got a firm bottom on your eggs, dollop over the rest of the mascarpone, then little bits of the remaining 'nduja. Sprinkle over the rest of the cheese and place under the grill for 4–5 minutes until the cheese is melted and the frittata is just cooked in the middle (though a little soft and runny is no bad thing). Allow to rest for 5 minutes, then transfer to a large plate if you can or serve straight from the pan.

PANCETTA, POTATO, RADICCHIO & SAGE FRITTATA

This is a great way to use up leftover jacket potatoes, but boiled or roast would also work. If you can't find radicchio, use a couple of heads of chicory, or watercress would also be nice. Make sure you get the pancetta golden; the little crunchy nuggets are one of my favourite things about this.

Serves 4

1 tbsp olive oil

125 g/4½ oz cubed smoked pancetta or lardons

2 big handfuls of sage leaves, roughly chopped

½ head of radicchio, shredded

250 g/9 oz leftover cooked potatoes, roughly sliced or chopped

8 eggs, beaten

80 g/3 oz/¾ cup Gruyère, Comté or Asiago cheese, grated

Salt and pepper

Preheat the grill to high. Warm the oil in a wide, ovenproof frying pan over a medium heat and fry the pancetta for 3–4 minutes until it's coloured and begins to release its fat.

Stir in the sage and radicchio and keep stirring until it begins to turn brown, wilt and soften, then fold in the potatoes so they get nicely covered in pancetta fat, trying not to break them up too much.

Season the eggs generously, then pour into the pan. Stir briefly to incorporate everything and cook gently for 3–4 minutes until you can see that the bottom is firm (the top will still be runny).

Once you've got a firm bottom on your eggs, sprinkle over the cheese and put under the grill for 4–5 minutes until the cheese is melted and the frittata is just cooked in the middle (though a little soft and runny is no bad thing). Allow to rest for 5 minutes, then transfer to a large plate if you can or serve straight from the pan.

SUMMERY TOMATO, BASIL & MOZZARELLA FRITTATA

This is the perfect dish for when your tomatoes are looking a little tired and squidgy. If you can get hold of the coloured heirloom ones, they make this a really striking dish. This makes a slightly wetter frittata than the previous ones owing to the tomatoes, but that's what I love about it – just like the tomatoes, it's super-juicy. A bit of toast to soak it up and you're in lunch heaven.

Serves 4

2 tbsp olive oil, plus extra for drizzling

50 g/1¾ oz/½ cup grated Parmesan cheese

8 eggs, beaten

125 g/4½ oz/1 cup grated cooking mozzarella

2 large handfuls of basil or Greek basil leaves, roughly chopped, plus extra to serve

300 g/10½ oz tomatoes of different colours and sizes, thinly sliced

Salt and pepper

Preheat the grill to high. Warm the oil in a wide, ovenproof frying pan over a medium heat. Stir the Parmesan into the eggs, then season and pour into the warm pan.

Cook gently for 3–4 minutes until you can see that the bottom is firm (the top will still be runny), then sprinkle over the mozzarella, followed by the basil and finally the tomato slices. Season the top of the tomatoes with a little salt and pepper, drizzle with a little oil, and put under the grill for 4–5 minutes until the tomatoes are coloured on the edges and the frittata is just cooked in the middle (though a little soft and runny is no bad thing). Allow to rest for 5 minutes, then transfer to a large plate if you can or serve straight from the pan. Tear over a little extra basil to serve.

FRIED RICE WITH CRISPY EGGS & SMACKED CUCUMBER

The ultimate comfort food. The key to crispiness here is leftover rice that's spent a night in the fridge, so this is the perfect lunch for the day after curry night. I suggest starting with a little curry paste and gradually adding more, depending on how much spice those taste buds can handle. I've written this for two as that's what fits in one pan. Do double the quantities if you want, but perhaps do it in two pans or in batches: you gotta get that pan-contact.

Serves 2

2 tbsp sunflower oil

400 g/14 oz/2½ cups cooked white or brown rice

1–2 tbsp Thai red curry paste

3 tsp light soy sauce

2 tsp fish sauce

4 spring onions, sliced, green and white parts separated

SMACKED CUCUMBER

1 cucumber

1 small garlic clove, peeled

1½ tsp caster sugar

2 tsp rice wine vinegar

1 tsp light soy sauce, plus extra to taste

2 tsp chilli oil, such as Chiu Chow, optional

CRISPY FRIED EGGS

1½ tbsp vegetable oil

2 eggs

Make the smacked cucumber first. Bash it with a rolling pin – don't pulverise – just until cracks appear on the surface. Slice in half lengthways and scrape out the seeds with a teaspoon, then cut into large diagonal chunks. Place in a colander over a bowl and sprinkle over ½ teaspoon of salt. Toss, then leave for at least 10 minutes while you get on with everything else.

Grate the garlic into a large mixing bowl and add all the remaining cucumber dressing ingredients, stirring until the sugar dissolves. Add the chilli oil if you fancy spicing things up. Set to one side.

To make the fried rice, stir the oil into the rice so every grain is covered. Heat a wok or large frying pan over a medium-high heat. As soon as the pan is super-hot, spread out the rice in an even layer in the pan, pushing it up the sides if you're using a wok. Leave the rice, undisturbed, for 6–8 minutes until the bottom is golden (stick a spoon underneath to check). It might snap and crackle a bit but don't worry.

Stir in 1 tablespoon of the curry paste, the soy sauce, fish sauce and spring onion whites, breaking the rice into bits with your spoon as you go. Taste and add more curry paste if you wish and adjust the seasoning with a little extra soy sauce if it needs it. Take off the heat and cover the pan with a clean tea towel to keep warm while you fry the eggs.

Drain the cucumber chunks of any remaining liquid, give them a quick dry with a clean tea towel and add to the dressing bowl. Mix well.

Finally, to fry the eggs, warm a small frying pan over a medium-high heat and add the vegetable oil. Once hot, crack in the eggs and fry until golden and crisp on the edges and cooked to your liking.

Sit an egg on top of the rice, with the cucumber piled next to it. Spoon over any leftover dressing and sprinkle with the spring onion greens.

Take Your Time with it

THE ADDED EXTRAS

BABA GANOUSH

This is smooth, smoky, silky, pillowy heaven. And the best bit is it takes no skill or effort whatsoever to get you there. It's traditionally made by charring the aubergines over a flame but since discovering this super-quick version, I've never looked back. All it needs is some warm **flatbreads (p.155)** and a good sprinkle of delicious **dukkah (p.150)**, or get your raw veg in there or spoon it over salads.

Makes about 610 g/1 lb 5 oz (VE)

1 large or 2 small aubergines, approx 500 g /1 lb 2 oz

75 ml/2¾ oz olive oil, plus extra for drizzling

1 small garlic clove, roughly chopped

2 tbsp tahini

Juice of 1 small lemon

A handful of parsley or mint leaves (or a mix), roughly chopped

Salt and pepper

Preheat the grill to high. Prick the aubergines a couple of times with a fork, then set on a baking tray under the grill and cook, turning 3 or 4 times until the outside is evenly blackened and they feel crisp on the outside and very soft on the inside when squeezed. This should take about 15–20 minutes.

Remove from the oven and allow to cool for a few moments before splitting open and using a spoon to scrape out the flesh into a sieve – try to shave as close to the skin as possible as this is where you find the smokiness (I like to add in the skin of half of one for extra smokiness). Drain in a sieve for just a couple of minutes to get rid of any excess juices.

Put the aubergine, ¾ teaspoon of salt and everything else except the herbs in a food processor or blender and whizz until fine and whippy. Stir in the herbs and check the seasoning. You may want to add more lemon juice too.

Will keep for at least a week in an airtight container in the fridge.

GOLDEN BEETROOT & TAHINI DIP

This is the most fantastic stuff, basically hummus without the chickpeas – if you can imagine that. The tahini gives it an amazing whippy texture while the golden beets lend a deep, earthy sweetness. Eat it as you would hummus (i.e. with EVERYTHING).

Tip: Use any colour beets you can get your hands on but the red ones do create the most fabulous colour... try this with **falafel (p.100)**.

Makes about 650 g/1 lb 7 oz

300 g/10½ oz golden beetroots, scrubbed
1 garlic clove, roughly chopped
5 tbsp tahini
4 tbsp lemon juice (about 1½ lemons)
4 tbsp water
175 ml/6 fl oz/¾ cup olive oil
Salt and pepper

Preheat the oven to 220°C fan/200°C/425°F/gas mark 7. Wrap the beets individually in foil, put on a baking tray and roast in the oven for 1 hour, or boil (unwrapped) for 30–40 minutes, depending on size. They're done when you can easily insert the tip of a sharp knife.

Peel while still warm, either under cold running water or wearing gloves (definitely advisable!), then leave to cool.

Put the beetroot and garlic in a food processor or blender along with ½ teaspoon of salt and blitz until finely chopped. Add all the other ingredients and blitz for a few minutes until you have a smooth, creamy sauce. Have a taste and adjust the seasoning to your liking.

Will keep for at least a week in an airtight container in the fridge.

Makes approx 325 g /11½ oz

1 small garlic clove, crushed with a pinch of salt
50 g/1¾ oz watercress, roughly chopped
40 g/1½ oz parsley, leaves and fine stalks, roughly chopped
10 g/¼ oz dill fronds, roughly chopped
10 g/¼ oz mint leaves, roughly chopped
2 spring onions, roughly chopped
2½ tsp white wine vinegar
1 tsp olive oil
200 g/7 oz/¾ cup Greek yogurt
Salt and pepper

WATERCRESS TZATZIKI

We've all tried the cucumber version, but how about the watercress version? Watercress is full of vitamins, this dip is a nutritional powerhouse. It's also one of my all-time favourites as it goes with everything, most especially tomatoes, fried eggs, smoked fish, curries and grilled meat.

Put all the ingredients except the vinegar, oil and yogurt in a food processor or blender and pulse-blitz until finely chopped. Add the vinegar, ½ teaspoon of salt and the oil, pulse-blitz just to incorporate, then transfer to a large bowl. Stir in the yogurt and season with pepper and a little more salt if you feel it needs it.

Will keep for at least a week in an airtight container in the fridge.

MUHAMMARA

Holy moly, this stuff is ADDICTIVE. It's very typical of Syria and Turkey and is basically a party in your mouth. If you've never made it before I highly recommend you give it a go.

If you happen to be making this in the summer when peppers are at their best, then definitely make it with the long pointy ones as they have a sweeter flavour than the Dutch ones. You'll probably need about 600 g/1 lb 5 oz of uncooked ones and you can omit the honey. If you don't have the time for all that, though, the quality of jarred ones is pretty high – we're all about speed 'n' ease around here! You ideally want the peppers to be in brine, but if you can only find the slightly vinegared ones (I recommend having a little nibble to check before starting), then leave out the vinegar in the recipe.

Makes about 650 g/1 lb 7 oz

150 g/5½ oz/1¼ cups walnuts

1½ tsp cumin seeds

1 garlic clove, crushed with a
    pinch of salt

325 g/11½ oz (drained weight)
    roasted and skinned red
    peppers from a jar, rinsed of
    brine

2 tsp Turkish pepper flakes (pul
    biber) or 2 pinches of regular
    chilli flakes

1 tsp smoked paprika

3 tsp runny honey

150 ml/5 fl oz/⅔ cup olive oil

1 tbsp red wine vinegar,
    optional, see intro above

Salt and pepper

Put the walnuts into a large frying pan and cook over a medium-low heat, moving the pan frequently, for 3–5 minutes until they've taken on a little colour, then tip onto a plate and leave to cool. Gently toast the cumin seeds in the same pan for 30 seconds until fragrant, then remove to cool.

Put everything in a food processor or blender, adding ¾ teaspoon of fine salt, and pulse-blitz to your preferred texture – I like mine a bit chunky but some people like it smooth. Have a taste and adjust the seasoning to your liking.

Will keep for at least 10 days in an airtight container in the fridge.

AVOCADO GREEN GODDESS

Makes about 325 g/11½ oz/

4 anchovy fillets, optional

3 spring onions, roughly chopped

½ garlic clove, finely crushed with a pinch of salt

A handful of parsley leaves, finely chopped

A few sprigs of tarragon, finely chopped

2 handfuls of basil leaves, roughly chopped

1 ripe avocado, halved, stoned and peeled

3 tbsp Greek yogurt

2 tsp Worcestershire sauce, optional

Zest and juice of 1 lemon

I like to think of this as the love child of guacamole and the classic Caesar. It certainly deserves its mythological name. It's as versatile as sauces get. Spoon it over a crisp green salad as you would a dressing, dress a chicken salad, dip your crisps into it, eat with fried eggs or serve with grilled veg and some feta – your options are endless.

Tip: Vegetarians and vegans can forego the anchovy and Worcestershire sauce and vegans can also substitute the yogurt.

Combine all the ingredients in a food processor or blender and blitz until smooth. Add a few splashes of water to loosen – it's better for dipping when it's thick, but you probably want it a little looser for dressing a salad. Have a taste and adjust to your liking – you may want to add more lemon or Worcestershire sauce.

Will keep for at least a week in an airtight container in the fridge.

SMOKED MACKEREL PÂTÉ

Makes about 425 g/1 lb

250 g/9 oz smoked mackerel fillets, skinned and deboned

125 g/4½ oz/½ cup crème fraîche or Greek yogurt

3 spring onions, chopped

A large handful of dill or parsley (or a mix), chopped

2 tsp Dijon mustard or horseradish sauce

Zest and juice of ½ lemon

Salt and pepper

I've yet to meet someone who doesn't love this dish passionately, even those who are a bit funny about strong fishy flavours. And the best thing? It's child's play. What's more, quantities really don't matter. It goes well with everything: inside a jacket potato, on toast with a soft-boiled egg and celery sticks, or with lots of crunchy veg to dip into it.

Tip: Great for parties too for when you need big bowls of dip or something to smoosh on a cracker to make a canapé.

Combine all the ingredients with a fork in a bowl and season to taste. You might want to add more lemon juice. Add a splash of water if your crème fraîche is very thick.

Will keep for at least a week in an airtight container in the fridge.

TONNATO SAUCE

Serves 4

4 anchovy fillets

1 garlic clove, roughly chopped

1½ tbsp capers, soaked if salted

2 egg yolks

1½ tsp Dijon mustard

Juice of ½ lemon

1½ tbsp red wine vinegar

220 g/8 oz good-quality tuna in oil (150 g/5½ oz drained weight)

125 ml/4 fl oz/½ cup olive oil (or a mix of olive and vegetable oil)

Salt and pepper

This is the ultimate, refined, yet versatile, lunchtime sauce. I like to serve it with a **quick salade niçoise (p.44)**, or spread in a sandwich with leftover roast chicken and a big tomato slice. The Italians eat it with cold roast veal or pork, which I'd also enthusiastically recommend.

Put the anchovy fillets, garlic and capers in a food processor or blender (or use a hand blender) and blitz until everything is finely chopped (I'm looking at you, garlic), then add the rest of the ingredients except half the tuna and the oil. Whizz until fine. Pulse-blitzing, add the oil, little by little, then blend until smooth. It should be the consistency of single cream. Fold in the remaining tuna, taste and adjust the seasoning to your liking – you may want to add more lemon or vinegar too.

Will keep for at least a week in an airtight container in the fridge.

TAHINI SAUCE

Makes 150 g/5½ oz

1 garlic clove, crushed with a pinch of salt

4 tbsp tahini

Juice of 1 lemon

2 tbsp olive oil

Salt and pepper

This is the perfect accompaniment to so many things. Try with **falafel (p.100)**, in your **sabich sandwich (p.12)** or drizzle over your **kofte, (p.102)**. If you add more lemon to make it looser and a little honey to make it sweeter it becomes a great dressing for Middle Eastern-style salads too.

Put the crushed garlic in a small bowl and stir in the tahini. Squeeze in the lemon juice and stir – it will thicken considerably. Start off by stirring in 3 tablespoons of water and then keep adding more until it is the consistency of double cream. Don't worry if it starts to split, just keep stirring. Add the olive oil and season.

Will keep for at least two weeks in an airtight container in the fridge.

FOUR HUMMUS

You may have heard of this stuff. But did you know making your own is stupidly easy if you have a food processor or blender? Cooking chickpeas from dry is worth the effort if you get the time. I know it looks like a lot of oil in these recipes, but it's essential to creating that irresistibly smooth texture and flavour.

Makes about 600 g/1 lb 5 oz

1 garlic clove, crushed with a pinch of salt

1 x 400 g/14 oz can chickpeas, drained and rinsed

2 tbsp tahini

4 tbsp lemon juice (about 1½ lemons)

200 ml/7 fl oz/1 cup olive oil

2 tbsp water

Salt and pepper

PLAIN

What's to say here? Except I think my version is the best. That's it.

Put everything except the lemon juice, oil and water in a food processor or blender with a teaspoon of salt and blitz until finely chopped.

With the motor running, pour in the lemon juice, oil and water in a steady stream until fully incorporated and the hummus is smooth. Have a taste and adjust the seasoning to your liking.

Will keep for at least a week in an airtight container in the fridge.

Makes about 630 g/1 lb 6 oz

1 garlic clove, crushed with a pinch of salt

1 x 400 g/14 oz can chickpeas, drained and rinsed

2 tbsp tahini

4 tbsp lemon juice (about 1½ lemons)

200 ml/7 fl oz/1 cup olive oil

4 tbsp water

20 g/¾ oz parsley leaves, roughly chopped

5 g/⅛ oz dill fronds, roughly chopped

5 g/⅛ oz chives, roughly chopped

Salt and pepper

HERBY

This is my number one favourite of this genre. Fresh and fragrant and a brilliant way to use up old herbs in the fridge. Use whatever you can get hold of, just making sure you get a balance of strongly flavoured ones, such as dill or tarragon, and subtler ones, such as parsley.

Put the garlic, chickpeas and tahini in a food processor or blender with a teaspoon of salt and blitz until finely chopped. With the motor running, pour in the lemon juice, oil and water in a steady stream until fully incorporated and the hummus is smooth.

Add the herbs and pulse-blitz until they're finely chopped and distributed nicely. Taste and adjust the seasoning to your liking.

Will keep for at least a week in an airtight container in the fridge.

ROAST BEET & CUMIN

Makes about 800 g/1 lb 12 oz

300 g/10½ oz red beetroots

1 x 400 g/14 oz can chickpeas, drained and rinsed

1 large garlic clove, crushed with a pinch of salt

4 tbsp tahini

1 heaped tbsp cumin seeds, toasted

4 tbsp lemon juice (about 1½ lemons)

135 ml/4½ fl oz/½ cup olive oil

Salt and pepper

This makes a lot but as it lasts for a week you'll easily zoom through it. It's the most cheerful, uplifting dip you'll ever make. Roasting the beets really brings out their flavour, but you could boil or use pre-cooked ones, if you like.

Tip: Peeling is much easier and cleaner either under cold running water or wearing gloves.

Preheat the oven to 220°C/200°C fan/425°F/gas mark 7. Wrap the beets individually in foil, put on a baking tray and roast for 1 hour, or boil unwrapped for 30–40 minutes, depending on size. They're done when you can easily insert the tip of a sharp knife. Peel while still warm, then leave to cool.

Once the beets are cool, put everything except the lemon juice and oil in a food processor or blender along with a teaspoon of salt and blitz until finely chopped.

With the motor running, pour in the lemon juice and oil in a steady stream until fully incorporated and the hummus is smooth, adding a few splashes of water to loosen if needed. Check the seasoning and add more salt and lemon juice if you feel it needs it. Will keep for at least a week in an airtight container in the fridge.

ROAST CARROT

Makes about 900 g/2 lb

500 g/1 lb 2 oz carrots, peeled and cut into 3 cm/1¼in chunks

135 ml/4½ fl oz/½ cup olive oil, plus 1 tbsp for roasting

1 large garlic clove, crushed with a pinch of salt

1 x 400 g/14 oz can chickpeas, drained and rinsed

3 tbsp tahini

Zest of 1 orange and juice of ½

3 tbsp lemon juice (about 1 lemon)

3 tbsp water

Salt and pepper

If you love a roast carrot, you're going to be into this. Pure, unadultered, carroty heaven — and it's a super vibrant colour, too.

Preheat the oven to 200°C/180°C fan/400°F/gas mark 6. Spread the carrots out on a baking tray, toss with the tablespoon of oil and some seasoning. Roast in the oven for 20–25 minutes until crisp on the edges and slightly shrivelled, then allow to cool.

Once cool, put all the ingredients except the citrus juices, remaning oil and the water in a food processor or blender along with a teaspoon of salt and blitz until finely chopped. With the motor running, pour in all the remaining liquids in a steady stream until fully incorporated and the hummus is smooth. Check the seasoning before serving.

Will keep for at least a week in an airtight container in the fridge.

WHOLE EGG MAYO

This is an absolute game changer that I discovered way too late in life from a friend. Using whole eggs means no messing around with the yolks, no whites sitting in your fridge for years AND best of all, this is much more stable so it's a lot less likely to curdle. The resulting mayo is a little smoother and lighter, but I actually prefer its texture to yolks only, so no going back for me. Increase the amount of garlic to two cloves for something closer to aioli. If you like your mayo a bit thicker or don't have a food processor or blender, see the traditional by-hand version below.

Makes 425 g/15 oz (V)
  (2 small jars)

2 eggs, at room temperature

1 garlic clove, crushed with a pinch of salt

1 tsp Dijon mustard

Juice of ½ lemon

100 ml/3½ fl oz/½ cup olive oil

200 ml/7 fl oz/1 cup sunflower or groundnut oil

Salt

Put the eggs in a food processor and blitz for a minute, then add the garlic, mustard, ½ teaspoon of salt and half the lemon juice and blitz to combine for another minute.

Mix the oils in a jug, then, with the motor running, slowly add to the eggs in a thin, steady stream. After about half the oil is in, you should hear a change as the eggs begin to hold the oil, but just keep going until all the oil is in. Once all the oil has been incorporated and you have a lovely, thick emulsion, add the remaining lemon juice. Taste and add a little more salt and lemon juice if needed.

At this stage, you can stir in whatever herbs, pickles, hot sauce you like. Will keep, for about a week in an airtight container in the fridge.

Tip:
If your mayo has curdled or split, don't panic! Keep what you have made so far, transfer the split mix to a jug and your clean bowl. Add another egg yolk to the clean bowl and start adding the split mix in a very slow drizzle as you did earlier with the oil. As soon as it thickens, add any remaining oil and take a deep sigh of relief.

By hand:
Put the eggs in a small mixing bowl and whisk for a good minute, then add the garlic, mustard, ½ teaspoon of salt and half the lemon juice and whisk to combine.

Mix the oils in a jug, then slowly add them, a few drips at a time, whisking constantly. Once you're about a third of the way through, increase to a super-thin, steady trickle. You should feel the eggs begin to hold the oil and the mixture should start to thicken very slightly.

Increase adding the oil to a thin, steady stream, still whisking constantly. Add a couple of teaspoons or so of water to loosen if it's beginning to feel thick. Once all the oil has been incorporated and you have a lovely, thick emulsion, add the remaining lemon juice. Taste and add a little more salt and lemon juice if needed.

Will keep for about a week in an airtight container in the fridge.

CHEAT'S GREEN MAYO

Makes about 300 g/10½ oz

A small handful each of basil and parsley leaves

A pinch of tarragon leaves

A pinch of dill fronds

200 g/7 oz shop-bought mayonnaise

1 egg yolk

Juice of ½ lemon

½ tsp Dijon mustard

5 tbsp extra virgin olive oil

Salt and pepper

I absolutely love the satisfaction of making mayo from scratch but sometimes I don't have the time, patience or enough olive oil. So here's a recipe for glamorising the shop-bought stuff and giving it a flavour-freshener. Use whatever herbs you have – go easy on the strong ones.

Put the herbs in a food processor or blender and pulse-blitz until finely chopped. Add the mayonnaise, yolk, lemon and mustard and pulse until combined. With the motor running, drizzle in the oil until you have a lovely green emulsion. Season to taste and add more lemon, if you wish.

Will keep for at least 5 days in an airtight container in the fridge.

AQUAFABA VEGAN MAYO

Makes about 400 g/14 oz (VE)

100 ml/3½ fl oz/½ cup aquafaba

1 garlic clove, crushed

2 tsp Dijon mustard

2 tbsp cider vinegar

100 ml/3½ fl oz/½ cup extra virgin olive oil

200 ml/7 fl oz/1 cup sunflower or groundnut oil

Salt

Aquafaba is the chic name for the gloopy liquid from a can of chickpeas that can be whipped to a thick foam like eggs – perfect for vegans. It is truly a miracle substance that can even be used in all types of dishes – try it to believe it. You should be able to get enough of it from a 400 g/14 oz can of chickpeas: drain off the starchy liquid and use the chickpeas in one of my **hummus recipes (p.140)** or in the **chicken shawarma salad (p.106)**. I recommend using either a hand blender and a jug or a powerful blender as you need some serious whizzing to get it going.

Put the aquafaba, garlic, mustard, a teaspoon of salt and the vinegar in a jug and blitz with a hand blender (or use a decent blender) on its highest setting for a minute or so until completely incorporated.

Mix the oils in a jug, then with the blender running, slowly add to the aquafaba – initially just a few drips, slowly increasing to a thin, steady stream. Move the hand blender up and down to incorporate a little air if you can; only towards the end will it start to thicken. Once all the oil has been incorporated and you have a lovely, thick emulsion, have a taste and add a little more vinegar if needed.

At this stage, you can stir in whatever herbs, pickles, hot sauce you like. Will keep for 2 weeks an airtight container in the fridge.

FOUR PICKLES & KRAUTS

BREAD & BUTTER PICKLES

I've heard a few reasons why these are so-named, the most convincing one being their compatibility with their namesake. They improve everything they're eaten with – I'd highly recommend slipping them into all your sandwiches, salads, pâtés and cured meats. They last forever too, so making them is an excellent investment in your future. The liquid here works as a great pickle base, so make extra and throw in whatever crunchy veg you like.

Makes about 900 g/2 lb
  You'll need a 1-litre/
  1¾-pint/4-cup jar or 2 x
  500-ml/17-fl oz/2-cup jars
  for this*

1 kg/2 lb 4 oz cucumber or
  gherkins, ends discarded

1 onion, sliced

125 g/4½ oz/½ cup caster
  sugar

200 ml/7 fl oz/1 cup cider
  vinegar

1 tbsp coriander seeds

2 tsp celery seeds

¼ tsp ground turmeric

¼ tsp chilli flakes

1 heaped tbsp yellow
  mustard seeds

1 star anise

Salt

Thoroughly wash your cucumber. Using your sharpest knife, a mandolin or the medium slicing attachment in a food processor, slice the cucumber – you want the pieces about 3–5 mm/⅛–¼in thick. Put in a colander over a bowl with the onion, toss with 1 tablespoon of salt and leave for at least 1 hour but no longer than 3 hours to drain.

Meanwhile, put the sugar, vinegar and spices in a pan and bring to a simmer, stirring until the sugar dissolves. Take off the heat and leave to cool.

Put the cucumber and the onion in a bowl and toss with the pickling liquid before transferring to your sterilised jars. Push the cucumber under the liquid, then seal and leave for at least 4 hours before eating. Will last a good month in the sealed jar in the fridge.

* Sterilise the jars and their lids by scrubbing them with soapy warm water and drying them for 15 minutes in the oven at 180°C/160°C fan/350°F/gas mark 4.

Makes about 250 g/9 oz

6 tbsp white wine, red wine or cider vinegar or lime juice

3 tsp caster sugar

2 red onions, finely sliced

Salt

ADDITIONAL FLAVOURS, OPTIONAL:

Bay leaves, star anise, coriander seeds, black peppercorns, dried oregano

Makes about 900 g/2 lb. You'll need a 1-litre/1¾-pint/4-cup jar or 2 x 500-ml/17-fl oz/2-cup jar for this*

VEGETABLES

2 carrots, peeled and halved lengthways

2 celery sticks

1 green chilli, halved and deseeded

1 head of fennel, tough outer layer discarded and halved lengthways

½ small cauliflower, core and leaves discarded

BRINE

250 ml/9 fl oz/1 cup white wine or cider vinegar

150 ml/5 fl oz/⅔ cup water

1 tbsp caster sugar

2 bay leaves

MARINADE

250 ml/9 fl oz/1 cup mild olive oil

1 tsp coriander seeds

½ tsp dried oregano

1 tsp fennel seeds

¼ tsp chilli flakes

2 garlic cloves, peeled and halved across the middle

2 bay leaves

 QUICK PICKLED ONIONS

Want the easiest way to impress someone with a plate of your food? Put these on top. They bring everything to life. They're amazing with most things but most especially with Mexican flavours, such as my **sweet potato tacos (p.104)** and **cheesy egg & sausage burrito (p.22)**. I also like them for jazzing up the **watermelon, mint & feta salad (p.50)**.

Warm the vinegar, sugar and ¼ teaspoon of salt in a small pan and stir until the sugar has just dissolved – don't allow to boil. Put the onions (and any additions) in a small bowl or sterilised jar and pour over the pickling liquid, pushing the onion down so it's submerged. Leave to cool, then serve.

Will keep for at least 2 weeks in an airtight container in the fridge.

GIARDINIERA

This vibrant little marinated veg pickle was introduced to Chicago by Italian immigrants, taking its place at the heart of their eating culture. You name it, they'll put giardiniera on it. And they're not wrong, it's just what we all need to bring our lunch to the flavour party. Try it on your avocado on toast, scattered over salad or with almost every porky dish: ham sandwiches, hot dogs and **prune & pork giant sausage rolls (p.122)**. Incidentally, I haven't included red pepper in this as I'm not into eating pepper raw, but do throw some in if you want.

Prepare the vegetables first. Slice everything into 3–5mm/⅛–¼in pieces on the diagonal. For the cauliflower, cut into 3–5mm/⅛–¼in slices, then run your knife through it once to break up the bigger bits. You basically want everything in roughly same-sized pieces. Put in a bowl.

Next, make the brine. Put all the ingredients in a pan and bring to the boil. Pour over the vegetables and stir well. It'll not quite cover, but don't worry. Allow to cool.

Meanwhile, make the marinade. Put all the ingredients in a pan and bring to a gentle simmer – don't boil – you just want everything to infuse into the oil. Take off the heat and leave to infuse.

Drain the veg, reserving the brine (you can save and reuse it). Return 4 tablespoons of the brine to the vegetables, then pour the infused oil over everything and stir well. Transfer to sterilised jars and leave to marinate for 24 hours before serving. Will keep for at least a month in the fridge.

The Added Extras

RED CABBAGE & CARROT KRAUT

Not only is this incredibly good for you but it brings a splash of colour to your plate. It's also very therapeutic to make, so put on some music and relax into it. You can make as little or as much as you want: keep in mind that you need 4 g/⅛ oz of fine salt per 200 g/7 oz of vegetables, so make sure after prepping them you have the weights given below.

Try to find nice, organic carrots for this as you'll really taste the difference. I like the flavour of straight-up kraut, but do add whatever flavours you like – there are some ideas below.

Makes about 900 g/2 lb. You'll need a 1-litre/1¾-pint/4-cup jar or 2 x 500-ml/17-fl oz/2-cup jars for this*

(VE)

750 g/1 lb 10 oz red cabbage (about 2), the outer leaves reserved, core discarded
400 g/14 oz carrots, peeled
Salt

ADDITIONAL FLAVOURS:

1 tbsp coriander, anise, fennel or cumin seeds
1 garlic clove, grated
A thumb of ginger, peeled and grated

Thoroughly wash your vegetables before prepping. Using your sharpest knife, a mandolin or the fine slicing attachment in a food processor, shred the cabbage and put in your biggest bowl or a very clean bucket. Use a coarse grater or food processor to shred the carrots and add to the cabbage.

Weigh the veg again to check you have the weights as above. Sprinkle over 23g/1oz of salt and add any extra flavours now (if using). With clean hands and gloves, start squeezing and massaging everything until it wilts and starts releasing liquid – this should take about 5–10 minutes. Cover the bowl or bucket with a clean tea towel and leave at room temperature for 30 minutes or up to 3 hours.

Pack tightly into your sterilised jars, pushing the veg down as you add each handful – you want it entirely submerged in it's own brine. Give it a final push down with your fist or a spoon. Lay the reserved outer cabbage leaves on top and press down again until there's a pool of brine in the cabbage leaf. Add any kind of weight and push down to compress even more. If there is not enough brine, top it up with a 2% salt solution (so dissolve 4 g/1/8 oz of salt in 200 ml/7fl oz/1 cup of water).

Cover the open top with a clean tea towel or cloth and secure with an elastic band so it can breathe but nothing can get in there. Sit on a plate in case of overspills. Leave in a dark place at a cool room temperature (about 18–20°C/64–68°F) for at least 5 days before eating, but for the best flavour, leave the kraut to ferment for 2–4 weeks; it will be faster in summer and slower in winter. Have a taste and stop the fermentation once you're happy with the flavour by storing in the fridge (either in the same jar or in smaller ones) where it will last at least 4–6 months.

* Sterilise the jars and their lids by scrubbing them with soapy warm water and drying them for 15 minutes in the oven at 180°C/160°C fan/350°F/gas mark 4.

FOUR DRESSINGS

EGG & ANCHOVY

This is an assertive dressing for anchovy-lovers. It's perfect for crunchy green leaves and **garlic croûtons (p.152)** or when you need something to pour over simply cooked green veg, such as asparagus. Despite the name, you can actually leave out the anchovies and substitute for 1 teaspoon of Worcestershire sauce. Add Parmesan to make this a classic Caesar dressing.

Tip: Lightly 'coddle' the egg (à la Julia Child) for 2 minutes if you're not keen on raw egg.

Makes about 175 ml/6 fl oz/
¾ cup

1 small garlic clove, crushed
  with a pinch of salt
1 egg yolk
6 anchovy fillets
2 tsp Dijon mustard
Juice of ½ lemon
1 tbsp red wine vinegar
135 ml/4½ fl oz/½ cup olive oil

Place all the dressing ingredients except the olive oil in a food processor or blender and blitz until finely chopped. Add the oil in a slow, steady steam until you have a thick sauce, adding a few splashes of water to loosen if you feel it needs it. Will keep for 3–5 days in an airtight container in the fridge.

CITRUSSY ORANGE

This dressing really wakes up your salads and is a great way of enhancing an otherwise straight-edged green salad. Try it with fresh fennel and avocado or with smoked mackerel. It's also great made with lemon zest or lime instead of orange. Absolutely use blood oranges when they are in season in the winter months.

Makes about 200ml/7fl oz/
  1 cup

Zest and juice of 1 small orange
1½ tbsp white wine vinegar
135ml/4½ fl oz/1½ cup extra
  virgin olive oil
Salt and pepper

Zest the orange straight into a small bowl, then cut in half and squeeze in the juice. Whisk in the vinegar and oil, season to taste and drizzle over your salad.

Will keep for 3 weeks in an airtight container in the fridge.

CAPER & RAISIN

This sweet and sour, salad-tickling fella is exceptionally moreish – beware! It works on all manner of vegetable dishes – roast and grilled, especially those with more subtle flavours, such as cauliflower, and is particularly good with **sweet & sour butter bean salad (p.56)**. This can all be chopped by hand if you don't want to get your blitzer out.

Makes about 175 ml/6 fl oz/ ¾ cup

1½ tbsp balsamic vinegar
1 tbsp red wine vinegar
30 g/1 oz/¼ cup raisins
½ garlic clove, roughly chopped
30 g/1 oz capers, soaked if salted
A handful of parsley or dill leaves (or a mix), roughly chopped
100 ml/3½ fl oz/½ cup olive oil

Combine the vinegars and raisins in a bowl for a few minutes while you prepare everything else.

Put the garlic, capers and herbs in a small food processor and pulse-blitz until finely chopped, then add the vinegars and raisins and blitz again to roughly chop. Finally, add the oil, pulse a few times to combine and then transfer to a bowl to serve.

Will keep for 3 weeks in an airtight container in the fridge; just get to room temp before using.

CREAMY MUSTARD

The recipe below is ideal for when you want a salad to accompany a piece of meat, such as steak or a pork chop – basically anything you'd normally serve with mustard. It loves a slightly bitter leaf, such as radicchio and chicory, but really, it's great with anything. I sometimes tame its punch with a couple of tablespoons of crème fraîche or soured cream and use it on potato salads or as a coleslaw dressing to eat with something from the barbecue. It also happens to be delicious with **sausage rolls (p.122)**.

Makes about 200 ml/7 fl oz/1 cup

1 tbsp Dijon mustard
2 tsp red wine vinegar
Juice of ½ lemon
135 ml/4½ fl oz/½ cup olive oil
Salt and pepper

Combine the mustard, vinegar and lemon juice, then slowly whisk in the oil so you achieve a bit of emulsification. Season to taste.

Will keep forever and ever in an airtight container in the fridge.

FOUR SEEDS & NUTS FOR SNACKING

Makes about 200 g/7oz

75 g/2¾ oz/½ cup whole
   almonds, skin on or skin off
25 g/1 oz/¼ cup blanched
   hazelnuts
25 g/1 oz/¼ cup shelled
   pistachios (or more hazelnuts)
2 tbsp coriander seeds
1 tbsp cumin seeds
1 tbsp fennel seeds
50 g/1¾ oz sesame seeds
1 tbsp sea salt flakes

DUKKAH

This Egyptian blend of nuts and spices is a secret weapon for lifting any savoury dish. Sprinkle over salads, plates of grilled vegetables, on your avocado toast, into a boiled egg or drench any of the **dips, (p.134–141)**. Make a jarful and thank me later.

Preheat the oven to 180°C/160°C fan/350°F/gas mark 4.

Spread everything except the salt on a greaseproof paper-lined baking tray and cook in the oven for 15–20 minutes until you can see the nuts are golden. Immediately transfer to a plate to cool.

Once cool, transfer to a small food processor, add the salt flakes and pulse-blitz until finely chopped (avoid over-blitzing as you want a little texture). Alternatively, you could use a pestle and mortar or spice grinder.

Will keep for at least a month in an airtight container.

Makes about 200 g/7 oz

100 g/3½ oz/½ cup pumpkin
   seeds
100 g/3½ oz/½ cup sunflower
   seeds
3 tbsp light soy sauce or tamari

SOY SEEDS

Do you like Marmite? Do you like snacking? OK, well these are for you. Dead simple and ridiculously moreish, these are one of my favourite things to mindlessly crunch down on while working, but they also add sparkle to your salads when you need some texture and a little salty ping.

Set a large frying pan over a medium heat and when hot, add the pumpkin seeds. Dry-fry, stirring only occasionally, until the pumpkin seeds start to pop, crackle and turn dark. Keep going for about 4–5 minutes until the majority of them are nicely coloured (but not black), then add the sunflower seeds to the pan and toast them for a minute or so until warmed through.

Pour in the soy sauce and immediately take off the heat, stirring constantly, until the seeds are evenly coated. Leave to cool.

Will keep for at least a month in an airtight container.

The Added Extras

Makes about 375 g/13 oz

125 g/4½ oz/1 cup jumbo oats

40 g/1½ oz/½ cup pumpkin seeds

60 g/2¼ oz/½ cup blanched hazelnuts, roughly chopped

25 g/1 oz/¼ cup sesame seeds

1 tsp fennel seeds

1½ tbsp coriander seeds

1½ tsp hot paprika

1 tbsp light soy sauce

4 tbsp olive oil

2 tbsp maple syrup or agave syrup

½ tsp garlic granules or MSG, optional

1 tbsp sesame oil

Salt

Makes about 300 g/10½ oz

3 x 400 g/14 oz cans chickpeas, drained and rinsed

3 tbsp olive oil

2 tsp ground cumin

2 tsp sweet paprika

1 tsp ground cinnamon

Salt

SAVOURY GRANOLA

Just like the **soy seeds (p.150)**, this makes the most addictive, irresistible snacking jar – I challenge you to actually save enough to put on your salads. This has a bit of a Mexican vibe so it is great with avocado. Please don't tell anyone but I like to give these a little extra oomph with garlic powder or MSG, but that's totally up to you.

Preheat the oven to 180°C/160°C fan/350°F/gas mark 4.

Combine everything except the sesame oil in a bowl with ½ teaspoon of salt and mix well. Spread out on a greaseproof paper-lined baking tray and bake in the oven for 20–25 minutes until golden, stirring once to prevent the edges from catching. Remove and immediately stir through the sesame oil and then leave to cool.

Will keep for at least 2 weeks in an airtight container.

CRISPY SPICED CHICKPEAS

We're all the same. We love a crunchy, salty snack and we wish we could find a nutritious one. Well... here it is, people! They're also brilliant on your salads or sprinkled over soups for crunch. Try with miso and gochujang for a big umami hit.

Tip: The chickpeas need to be very dry to get crispy, so use a clean tea towel to get them there.

Preheat the oven to 180°C/160°C fan/350°F/gas mark 4.

Put the chickpeas in a clean tea towel and rub gently to dry and remove as many of the chickpea skins as possible. It's not necessary to remove all the skins but try to get off as many as you can.

Combine all the other ingredients in a mixing bowl with ¾ teaspoon of salt, then stir in the chickpeas.

Tip the chickpeas onto a greaseproof paper-lined baking tray and spread into a single layer. Roast for about 35–50 minutes until crispy and dry, shaking the pan occasionally. The exact time can vary, so watch them closely in the final minutes and do a taste test – you want them dark golden brown but not very dark and hard. Season with extra salt, if desired. Allow to cool completely before storing; the chickpeas will crisp up even more as they cool. Will keep for at least a week in an airtight container.

FOUR CRUNCHY SALAD & SOUP ACCESSORIES

PANGRATTATO

Meaning 'grated bread' in Italian, these crunchy fried breadcrumbs were used as poor man's Parmesan for their ability to administer a dish with texture and finish it with a flourish. Pangrattato can be infused with all sorts of flavours – see the variations opposite – and makes a compelling addition to pasta, soup, risotto and salad dishes. Homemade fresh breadcrumbs are best, but shop-bought are fine too.

Makes 140g/5 oz

150 g/5½ oz day-old (or older) **sourdough bread**, crusts removed

2 tbsp **olive oil**

1 **garlic clove**, peeled and halved lengthways

½ tbsp **thyme leaves**, roughly chopped

Salt and pepper

Put the bread in a food processor (or chop finely by hand) and pulse-blitz until you have finer breadcrumbs.

Warm the oil and garlic in a large frying pan over a medium heat and, just as the garlic begins to colour, add the breadcrumbs and thyme and fry, stirring constantly, until the bread has an even golden colour. Season, discard the garlic, then scoop onto a plate to cool. Will keep for 3 days in an airtight container.

VARIATIONS

Chilli & lemon

Add ½ teaspoon of chilli flakes in place of the thyme and the zest of ½ lemon once the crumbs are cooling.

Anchovy & rosemary

Add 3 chopped anchovies with the garlic, crushing them into the pan so they melt in. Add 1 teaspoon of roughly chopped rosemary leaves in place of the thyme.

Fennel, oregano & chilli

Add 1 teaspoon of fennel seeds, ¼ teaspoon of dried oregano and ½ teaspoon of chilli flakes in place of (or as well as) the thyme.

GARLIC CROÛTONS

I'm not going to tell you what to do with these – you've got this – though I STRONGLY advise making the **panzanella (p.60)** if it's the summer or **paillard chicken with caesar salad (p.62)**. Remove the crusts if you're feeling fancy, but I tend not to bother.

Tip: Add 3 tablespoons of grated Parmesan cheese for a cheesy croûton (perfect for adding to the **pumpkin soup on (p.94)**.

Makes enough for 4 salad portions

200 g/7 oz stale sourdough bread

3 tbsp olive oil

2 small garlic cloves, roughly chopped

Salt and pepper

Preheat the oven to 200°C/180°C fan/400°F/gas mark 6. Tear the bread into small chunks and put on a large baking tray. Drizzle with the oil, sprinkle with the chopped garlic and season with salt and pepper, then toss it all together with your hands, making sure the bread is nicely coated. Pop in the oven for 10–15 minutes (depending on the size of the pieces), stirring once or twice, until golden and crunchy. Cool on the baking tray.

Will keep for 3 days in an airtight container.

ZA'ATAR PITTA CHIPS

Za'atar is a Middle Eastern spice blend that is full of fragrant flavours. These bread chips are the ultimate vessel for dips, especially **golden beetroot & tahini dip (p.137)** and they're great to have at hand to lend a herby hum and crunchy scoop when eating salads such as **watermelon, feta & pickled onion salad (p.50)**.

Makes enough for 4 (VE)

6 pitta breads, white or wholemeal

100 ml/3½ fl oz/½ cup olive oil

1 tsp dried oregano

1 tsp dried thyme

3 tsp sumac

3 tsp sesame seeds

Salt

Preheat the oven to 200°C/180°C fan/400°F/gas mark 6. Line 2 large or medium baking trays with greaseproof paper.

Pop the pittas in the toaster for a few seconds to make them easier to slice. Cut each of the pittas into six even triangles, carefully open each one, and separate at the attached end, so that you get 2 triangles from each.

Combine all the remaining ingredients and ¾ teaspoon of salt in a mixing bowl and toss with the pitta triangles. Spread them out on the lined trays, a little piled up is fine. Bake the oven for 7–9 minutes until just turning golden (they'll harden as they cool on the tray).

Will keep for at least a week in an airtight container.

FIVE-SEED CRISPBREAD

This is a miracle of chemistry. The magic of sticky chia seeds means that you need no gluten or fat to bind it together, so you're putting 100% wholesomeness straight into your mouth. Despite this, they're incredibly seedy and delicious, especially plunged into one of my **hummus recipes (p.140–141)** and **muhammara (p.134)**. This makes a big batch but they won't last long...

Makes about 300 g/10½ oz

85 g/3 oz chia seeds
60 g/2¼ oz/½ cup sunflower seeds
65 g/2¼ oz/½ cup pumpkin seeds
85 g/3 oz/¾ cup sesame seeds
30 g/1 oz/¼ cup linseeds
250 ml/9 fl oz/1 cup water
Salt

Preheat the oven to 150°C/130°C fan/300°F/gas mark 2. Line 1 large or 2 smaller baking trays with greaseproof paper.

Combine all the ingredients in a bowl with ½ teaspoon of salt and leave for at least 15 minutes to give the chia time to swell.

Spread out on the lined baking tray(s), and use a large metal spoon to smooth the surface. Take time to spread it evenly to the corners and make it nice and smooth. You can cover the top with another piece of greaseproof paper and use a small rolling pin to do this too (remove the top piece of paper before baking). The thinner you can get it (without being able to see the paper below), the crispier it will be.

Bake in the oven for 35 minutes, then remove and carefully turn the whole thing over before returning to the oven for another 25 minutes. Once ready, it should be nice and crispy and the pumpkin seeds slightly coloured. Leave to cool on the baking tray(s), then break into shards to serve.

Will keep for at least two weeks in an airtight container

FIVE-MINUTE FLUFFY FLATBREADS

I think the title sells these. Eat with **chicken shawarma salad (p.106)** or **falafel (p.100)**. You can grill them or fry them in a big splash of olive oil. If you are using oil, keep the heat medium-high, otherwise the oil will burn.

Makes 4

250 g/9 oz/2 cups self-raising flour, plus extra to dust

1 tsp baking powder

180 g/6¼ oz/¾ cup Greek or other natural thick yogurt

A splash of olive oil (if frying)

Salt

Combine the flour, baking powder and 1 teaspoon of salt in a bowl and stir in the yogurt. Using your hands, bring the mix together, then tip onto a lightly floured work surface and knead for a minute. Divide and shape into four equal balls and put to one side for a moment.

Set a griddle pan over a high heat (or a frying pan with the oil over a medium-high heat). Roll out each ball on a lightly floured work surface to make a flatbread about 20 cm/8in diameter.

When the pan is super-hot (medium-hot if frying), cook the first flatbread for about 30–40 seconds until char marks appear, then turn over and cook the other side for a further 30-40 seconds. Keep the cooked ones wrapped in a clean tea towel while you cook the rest. Serve warm.

INDEX

GLOSSARY (UK/US)

Aubergine/eggplant
Autumn/fall
Beetroot/beet
Bicarbonate of soda/baking soda
Broad beans/fava beans
Butter beans/lima beans
Caster sugar/superfine sugar
Cavolo nero/Tuscan kale (or black kale)
Celeriac/celery root (only mentioned in intro on p39, not actually used
in any recipes)
Chestnut mushrooms/cremini mushrooms
Chickpeas/garbanzo beans
Chilli/chili
Chilli flakes/crushed red pepper flakes
Chinese leaf cabbage/napa cabbage (written as Chinese cabbage in
recipe on p114)
Coriander (fresh)/cilantro
Courgette/zucchini
Flaked almonds/slivered almonds
Fridge/refrigerator
Frying pan/skillet
Greaseproof paper/wax paper
Grill/broiler (grill/broil)
Groundnut oil/peanut oil
Hand blender/immersion blender
Kitchen paper/paper towel
Little Gem lettuce/Boston lettuce (or butter lettuce)
Mince (meat)/ground meat
Natural yogurt/plain yogurt
Packet/package
Passata/sieved (strained) tomatoes
Pepper (red, green, orange or yellow)/bell pepper
Pine kernels/pine nuts
Pitta bread/pita bread
Plain flour/all-purpose flour
Prawn/shrimp (also king prawn/jumbo shrimp)
Rasher (bacon)/strip
Rocket/arugula
Self-raising flour/self-rising flour
Sieve/strainer
Soured cream/sour cream
Spring onions/scallions
Tea towel/dish towel
Wholemeal bread/wholewheat bread
Wholemeal flour/wholewheat flour

ACKNOWLEDGEMENTS

The hugest of thank yous to my agent, Elly James, for being so supportive and encouraging, this wouldn't exist without your bolstering. To Cara at Pavilion for believing in everyone's appetite for lunch and for getting me on the writing train. And to the rest of the Pavilion team, Stephanie Evans, Ellen Simmons and Laura Russell.

And to the Let's do Lunch shoot crew, Sam Harris for his calm presence and truly exceptional way of looking at things, to Rachel Vere for her beautiful hands and great taste, and Eleanor Silcock for her brilliant ideas and sauce swooshing skills.

My parents also need to take a lot of credit for this book. They have always given me free reign in their kitchen, praised every single thing I've ever cooked and loudly cheered for me along every step of my career. And to my sister, who has cheerfully tried everything.

To the wonderful Ollie, who has been my head (and not very impartial) taste tester. And James, who has taught me so much about cooking and eating just by sitting at his dinner table.

And to all my incredible friends who have all contributed so much to this. Sam and Su for being such supportive and hungry neighbours and knowing just when I needed encouragement. And to the unbelievable testing team headed up by the extraordinary Norah, who tested one of my recipes every day for two weeks. Thank you Cassy, Lennie and Sophie, Cherry, Dan and David.